Jacquie McTaggart
www.theteachersdesk.com
mctag@indytel.com
(319) 334-3585

From the Teacher's Desk

Y0-CZP-417

Deborah

"To the best instructional Coach in the District,

Jacquie McTaggart

Booklocker.com. Inc.
2003

Early readers' praise

FROM THE TEACHER'S DESK

Jacquie McTaggart provides heartwarming, down-to-earth advice and information based on over four decades of experience – indispensable for parents and those who care about children and our schools.

Bill Asenjo, PhD, CRC
Writer, Consultant

Jacquie McTaggart combines 42 years of classroom experience with intelligence and a loving heart.
She offers parents pro-active guidance for making every school year a successful one. McTaggart knows that the AD/HD-Ritalin issues aren't simply black and white, but largely gray. She explains how and why teachers and parents must join forces to find the perfect 'shade' for each child. A "must-read" for those who are rearing or teaching kids that march to a *different drummer*.

Alaine Benard
Author – Columnist – Educator - Mother
www.ADHD.StormWatch.com

Every once in awhile a book comes along that is so absolutely practical an announcement should be made in every newspaper throughout the country. *From the Teacher's Desk* meets the criteria of excellence. If you are going to read just one book this year, **make it this one!**

In her book, Jacquie McTaggart reduces 42 years of teaching experience into a compendium that will enlighten and entertain teachers, aspiring teachers, parents, administrators, and those who legislate today's educational policies. *From the Teacher's Desk* is more than a timely publication for education's stakeholders – it is a joy to read.

Dr. James Kelly
Professor of Teaching
University of Northern Iowa

With humor and compassion, *From the Teachers Desk* provides a textbook analysis of the joys of teaching. Jacquie is an incredibly gifted writer who weaves her 42 years of teaching through unique stories based on individual classroom experiences. This is a must-read book that promises to inspire parents, teachers, and policy makers.

Kitty Rehberg
Iowa State Senator

From the Teacher's Desk is an honest reflection on current issues important to educators across this country. Parents, policy makers, and the tax paying public should read it.

Christie Vilsack
First Lady of Iowa

As a teacher educator, I have drawn on Jacquie's vignettes to reinforce various concepts with pre-service educators. They appreciate her experience and her honesty as she shares the complex world of their future careers. They often recognize situations they have observed within school situations, and her dialogue leads to greater understanding. Jacquie has blended theory and practice into a humorous, enlightening, and enjoyable read. It holds appeal for a variety of audiences.

Cynthia Waters, CFCS
Assistant Professor in Education
Upper Iowa University

From the Teacher's Desk

Jacquie McTaggart

To the 1500 students who overlooked my shortcomings, showed me how to teach, and taught me how to dream.

J.Mc.

ACKNOWLEDGEMENTS

Although I wrote this book alone, hundreds of people contributed. To each of them I offer my sincere thanks. The journey started with sacrifices made by my mother and late father. Sacrifices that allowed me to attend college and earn the coveted title of "TEACHER." It ended when Richard and Angela from Booklocker took me by the hand and led me through the incredible maze of publishing.

In between, more than 1500 students showed me when to talk and when to listen. They taught me how to imagine, and how to dream. They gave me wonderful memories, and left footprints on my heart. The parents of those 1500 kids entrusted me with their most prized possession and they extended their hands to me in cooperation, assistance, and yes - friendship. My students and their parents ultimately gave me a wonderful gift. They provided me with the experiences and gave me the incentive to write this book.

During my 42-year teaching career I had the good fortune of working with hundreds of master teachers and outstanding administrators. Together they helped and inspired me. They demonstrated good teaching, and they invited me to follow their path. They were the wind beneath my wings, and I give them my thanks.

I owe a special thank you to my husband. For 40 years Carroll climbed through barbed wire fences in search of monarch caterpillars. He made annual car trips to secure *fertile* chicken, duck, and goose eggs so that my first graders could experience the wonderment of hatching. He built storage boxes, bookcases, and puppet theatres. He endured my shortcomings, comforted me in times of failure, and rejoiced in my successes. And - for the most part - he refrained from complaining about the hundreds of hours I spent writing this book. I could ask for nothing more.

Finally, I want to publicly acknowledge my love and appreciation to sons Mark and Sean, and daughters-in-law Leslie and Linda. Without their encouragement and support, this book would not have been completed. They held my hand (figuratively) as I struggled through the disappointment of publishers' rejection letters, and urged me to forge ahead. I am thankful they didn't allow me to quit when the going got rough. The destination has made the journey worthwhile.

CONTENTS

MEET THE TEACHER

As I sat in my computer room staring at my 1,119th game of solitaire, I thought about all the kids at school who were meeting their teacher for a brand new school year. I could smell their clean hair, see their new outfits, hear the sounds of their laughter, and sense their feelings of excitement-mixed with twinges of apprehension.

It was my first "official" day of retirement, and I was already homesick for the classroom. I was not simply missing the exhilaration that earlier teaching retirees had told me to expect. I was experiencing a get-me-the-Valium depression.

I silently wondered if I had made a major "boo-boo" the prior spring when I accepted the district's financial incentive package designed to encourage early retirement. I had accepted the offer because I wanted to leave the classroom while I was still productive. I did not want to end my career as a crotchety old biddy that fell asleep at her desk during sharing time, and waddled to her car promptly at 4:00 p.m. in order to "rest up" for another day.

I had been fortunate to earn a reputation in the community for being a teacher who demanded maximum student effort, maintained discipline, enjoyed a good rapport with her students, and had FUN doing it. I did not want to tarnish that image by pressing my luck and hanging on too long. Yes, my head said that I had done the right thing.

My heart, however, was giving me a message that sounded much different. My heart said I must have been totally out of my mind when I wrote that letter of resignation. I had always loved teaching, and everything it entailed. Well, almost everything. The hours were long and the pay was short. The required paperwork (ordered in triplicate) was a pain in the posterior. Staff development sessions were usually ineffective and often unrelated to the real world of kids or their learning. And the meetings were endless! Before school, after school, recess, lunch break, – it didn't matter. The principal set the time, and we met. But those things were just "fluff."

It was the real stuff that I was going miss. The thrill of hearing a six year old read a six-word sentence for the first time. The joy of receiving a beautiful hand crafted picture with an "I luv u" notation. The satisfaction derived from a student's "I GET IT!" grin. The excitement felt upon hearing a complimentary or appreciative comment from a parent. The generosity of a colleague who was willing to share a special artifact or a new idea that worked. The cooperation of a principal who was willing to listen to a question, offer a suggestion, or help solve a problem. Ah, yes. Those were the joys of teaching. Those were the things that mattered.

In 1958, at the age of 19 and a member of the last class allowed to teach with a two-year pre-professional certificate, I began my teaching career. My first teaching assignment was in the small rural community of Waukon, Iowa where I was entrusted with *thirty-six* first graders. I was extremely fortunate to start my teaching career in Waukon because it gave me the opportunity to become acquainted and learn from Mrs. Reher.

Mrs. Reher taught another section of first grade, and also happened to be the wife of the school superintendent. (I thought – in those days – that the Superintendent of Schools was God. So I guess that made her Mrs. God.) Anyway, Mrs. Reher was not only a master teacher. She was a master mentor. She taught me *how* to teach reading. She demonstrated how to be firm without showing anger. She showed me how to develop a good relationship with parents without being pushy, *or* being pushed over. But her best gift of all was her attitude about kids.

I first heard Mrs. Reher's philosophy the day before the kids were due to arrive for the new school year. I was going over my class list with her, and asking if she had any inside information about my soon-to-be students. She told me that one of my new students, "Terry Brown", had been in her first grade classroom the prior year, but was retained because he had not yet learned how to read. "However," she quickly added, "You must never give up on a child. They all are ready to learn at different times and they learn at different rates. Furthermore, kids may not remember what you tell them, but they'll remember how you make them feel."

As I listened, I knew there was a lot of truth in what she said. I didn't realize, however, that those very words would become embedded deeply, firmly, and permanently into my own philosophy of teaching. They did, in fact, accompany and guide me throughout my entire career. (Thank you, Mrs. Reher!)

Had I spent my entire forty-two year teaching career in Waukon, my last students would have been the *grandchildren* of the students in my first class. But I didn't! In the summer between my first and second year of teaching at Waukon, I met "Mr. Right." There was a problem, however. Mr. Right wasn't committing himself to the wedding band scenario. (In those days you got married, and then you lived together.) So, what was a gal to do? Move, of course. I had decided that such a drastic action would either make or break the relationship. I was prepared to take the risk.

The "move" took me 200 miles north to Albert Lea, Minnesota and a class of thirty-two first graders. One trip to Albert Lea was apparently enough to convince Mr. Right that a marriage license was cheaper than gas. We were married the following June and set up housekeeping in the small town of Elkader, Iowa. Because there were no teaching vacancies that year in Elkader, I drove fifteen miles and fifty-two curves (no, I'm not exaggerating) to my hometown of Strawberry Point. Once again, I taught first grade.

In 1962 a teaching position became available in Elkader, and you guessed it...another FIRST GRADE. That time I got to stay in the same community and the same classroom for four wonderful years. Then hubby's job caused us to move to Independence, Iowa.

By the time we made our move, I had earned my BA degree and given birth to son number one. Mark was two years old when we moved. I decided to teach part time.

I accepted a three-quarter-time position teaching emotionally disturbed six to eight year olds at the local Mental Health Hospital. We spent our days in a small brick building located on the hospital grounds. Kids ate and slept in an adjacent dormitory. If a child successfully completed three consecutive months of hospitalization without any major infractions in the dorm or at school, he was allowed to go home for a weekend visit – if his parents wanted him to. (Some did, and some didn't.) That job lasted one year. Those little kids needed a teacher who could love them unconditionally during the day, and leave their problems at the hospital when she went home for the evening. And that teacher wasn't me. The first part of the equation was no problem. Leaving their little troubled lives behind for sixteen hours *was* a problem. I wanted to go back to a "regular" classroom with regular kids and regular parents.

The following fall I took a third-grade teaching job in the Independence Public schools. Uh, oh. I'd been teaching for many years, but it had all been at the first grade level. I wondered what in the world you did with kids who already knew how to read!

Enter Mrs. Hatfield. Mrs. Hatfield was somewhat older than I in calendar years, but light years younger in spirit and vivaciousness. She was the teacher every third grader hoped for, and the one requested by nearly every parent. She expected high achievement from her students, and she got it. She treated her kids with respect, and in return she earned theirs. She believed in making learning fun without allowing her classroom to be transformed into a three-ring circus. She strongly believed that, given enough time and proper encouragement, *every* child could learn. And best of all, she was willing to take me by the hand and share her wisdom with me. (Thank you, Mrs. Hatfield!)

After two years of teaching third grade, a first grade position became available. I was asked if I might be interested. Yes, as a matter of fact, I was. I had enjoyed my two–year tenure with kids who could tie their own shoes, zip their own zippers, and work independently for more than two minutes. But, first grade was my passion. I was ready to go back.

I returned to teaching first grade in 1969, and remained there until my retirement at the end of the 2000-2001 school year. During that time the curriculum changed. Theories evolved. Innovations were introduced that were guaranteed to enhance the learning process. Many were subsequently discarded. Old terminology was eliminated. New "buzzwords" were formed. Some old challenges disappeared, and new ones surfaced. Classes became smaller. Problems loomed larger. Respect for the teacher diminished. School spending increased. Women joined the workforce in droves. Men took on moonlighting jobs. Divorce rates mushroomed. Single parenting became common. Immigration burgeoned. Programs were introduced to combat drugs, alcohol, and violence. Technological advancements irrevocably changed the course of education.

I changed buildings when our district departed from the neighborhood school concept and went to a "leveling" plan. The new configuration placed kindergarten through second graders in a building on the East side of town, and third through fifth graders in a school on the West side. A middle school housed sixth, seventh and eighth graders. Ninth through twelfth graders completed their education at Jefferson High School.

I changed rooms when the school configuration changed, and again when I was moved from an unbelievably tiny room to the largest room in the school. (I think it had something to do with the squeaky wheel getting the oil.) Much to my disgruntlement, I returned to that "unbelievably tiny room" for my last year after the administration decided to turn *my* room into a computer lab. (The wheel squeaked again, but this time no one listened.) So much for the benefits of longevity!

Teaching was a wonderful ride. But now the music had stopped. I had been put out to pasture (albeit by my own choice), and there was no gate to aid my escape. I might as well stay there and munch grass.

As I clicked on my 1,204th solitaire game, hubby stuck his head in the doorway of my office and said, "What's for lunch?" And without so much as a blink from my swollen red eyes I responded, "Do I look like Martha Stewart?" Zing.

"Honey," he said, "Let's sit down and plan that fall trip to the New England states that you've talked about for years. I think you need to get away." I quickly informed him that I didn't want to get away. I wanted to go back to teaching.

My husband reminded me that I had chosen to retire in the first place, and he didn't think it was feasible to reconsider at this juncture. He went on to suggest that I might enjoy increasing my volunteer hours with our church or any of the various organizations that I was involved in. I then explained (in my most sarcastic voice) that if I were going to work forty hours, I wanted to get paid for it. "Well fine," he retorted. "Go get a job as a Wal Mart greeter, or...or...write a book. See if I care." And with that, he turned on his heels and left. (Come to think of it, I wonder if he ever got lunch that day.)

"Hmmm. Maybe I should write a book," I mused. I had always enjoyed writing, and a few people had told me I was fairly good at it. But what kind of book would I write that anyone would possibly want to read? My favorite genre for leisure reading is True Crime stories. In fact, I might be tempted to trade any one of my eight grandkids in exchange for a chance to meet the queen of true crime writers - Ann Rule. But, my only involvement with any kind of trial has been in the form of an opinion e-mailed to Court TV. No, writing True Crime stories was definitely not a viable option. Mystery stories? The biggest mystery in my life has been finding a way to make our money stretch far enough to pay all the bills. Scratch out mystery. How about a novel filled with some hot and steamy romance? Nope. I'm 64 years old! My memory won't stretch that far back, and my imagination won't leap that far forward.

And then ......DRUM ROLL......it hit me. I would write about my passion – education. No, it wouldn't be one of those sickening renditions about how wonderful everything is in our schools today. Neither would it be a hatchet to chop out all the positive things we have going for us. And it would *not* be a philosophical pipedream guaranteed to "leave no child behind."

It would be about educational issues and parenting issues that affect the educational process. It would include the good, the bad, and the ugly. It would be an honest disclosure of my views about what we are doing well, and an examination of the areas where we can and should do better.

And that is how this book came to be. I offer you a window where you can look in and see what is happening. I suggest some recommendations for change. I extend an invitation for you to help.

Politicians need clearer vision and less hyperbole. Parents need to examine their learning environments, and their commitment to education. Educators need to continue their struggle to find a better way to educate all kids – regardless of intelligence, color, wealth, residence, or opportunities.

No single segment of society can expect to accomplish the monumental task of improving education by flying solo. We need each other. Can we count on you?

As you read this book you will notice that I am often critical of political rhetoric that deals with education and the legislative action that follows. I do not do this for the purpose of assigning blame or tagging a scapegoat with a "You're it" label. All criticism is leveled for the purpose of provoking thought and encouraging discussion. It is my hope that these discussions will result in a better understanding of how we can improve our learning environment and our schools. It's all about kids and how we can best prepare them to become contributing members of society.

It is important you understand that what I present to you as fact is exactly that. It has been documented and is irrefutable. When I express an opinion, I am sharing my personal feelings - based on experience. No doubt you will agree with some opinions, and disagree with others. That is your right.

All anecdotes and adult names in this book are factual. Student names and identifying information have been altered.

By my students I was taught, and because of them I reached higher.

-Michael F. O'Brien

2

READY, SET, GO

One evening during the early stages of writing this book, the phone rang. I answered and heard our youngest son, Sean, on the other end as well as our daughter-in-law, Linda. Sean asked that I get Dad on another phone because they had some news to share. Well, I may not be the sharpest tack in the box, but I figured their "news" meant a sibling for two-year old Max was on the way. When I heard my husband pick up the extension phone I said, "Let me guess. There's a baby on the way." Linda responded with, "Not exactly. We are expecting *babies.*" Whoopee! I'm going to be the grandma of twins.

So this chapter is for Sean and Linda, and all you parents out there who want to give your very young child a head start at learning.

At the beginning of a school year, any typical kindergarten class has a 1.2 years mental age difference between the highest and the lowest achieving students. Said another way, the highest achieving (not necessarily the "smartest") child performs at a level of one year and two months beyond that of the lowest performing child. If both children were to learn at exactly the same rate, beginning with the first day of school, the "late starter" would *never* catch up to the first one out of the gate.

In reality, the gap **widens** with every successive year in school. Those who enroll in kindergarten ready to learn, move ahead faster while the others fall farther behind. This knowledge suggests that we need to do everything we possibly can to provide the kinds of dialogue, activities, and experiences that will enable our child to be READY TO LEARN, once he enters school.

It would be nice if our kids arrived with a set of instructions and a hotline to call for help in case of "technical difficulties." But, they don't. However, child-rearing "experts" and early childhood teachers have pinpointed several ways by which we *can* provide our little ones with the skills that will allow them to start school on an equal footing with their peers. I'd like to share some of those ideas with you.

Communicate. From birth on, **talk** to and with your child as much as possible. Try to avoid "baby talk." Talk about the colors, size, and shapes of things. Make a conscientious effort to use what we call "positional" words such as *before, after, above, below, in front of, behind,* etc. **Listen** to your little one. Show interest in what he is trying to communicate. Laugh at his "corny" little tricks and early attempts to tease. **Respond** to his questions – even if you're not sure you're giving the correct answer! (He'll probably not remember the answer you give, but your attention to his question will fill a need.)

Read. Jim Trelease is the most highly regarded expert in this country on the benefits of reading to children. He indicates that reading to and with kids from an early age (beginning at nine months) is the single most important thing you can do to insure a successful reading experience once he enters school. Following are some tips that provide extra benefits when you read to your child.

Discuss the pictures on every page. Use voice inflection – in other words, "ham it up." If your child is three (or older), run your finger under each line of print as you read. If you're reading a book for the first time, stop at appropriate places and ask your child to predict what will come next. (Never, ever, ridicule his predictions.) Simply say, "Well, let's find out if our guess is the same as the author's choice," and proceed. When the book is completed, talk about it. And finally, never refuse to re-read a book if your child requests it – and he will! I know, sometimes you could just gag when he brings you the same book for the hundredth time and asks you to read it. But try to remember that some books become "real" to a kid. They're like special friends they can see again and again, and never tire of their company.

Rhyme. Inundate your little one with nursery rhymes, starting at birth. Some of you might choose to do rhymes orally by simply reciting the ones you are familiar with. Others might prefer to read rhymes from any of the beautifully illustrated nursery rhyme books available in all bookstores and online. And still others might choose to utilize tapes, CD's, or DVD's. ALL of these methods provide huge benefits. When your rhyme-conscious child reaches kindergarten and learns how to read the word "red", he will almost automatically know how to read *bed, fed, Ted*, etc. You get a lot of bang for your buck when you introduce your little one to the wiggly giggly world of rhyme.

Activities. Puzzles and age-appropriate games are wonderfully inexpensive activities to engage in with your toddler or pre-school child. Provide lots of big paper and drawing supplies for your little one to experiment with. Never miss an opportunity to count things and if possible, touch each thing as you count it. (This procedure is much more valuable than simply reciting the numbers from one to ten.) The same suggestion applies to the alphabet. Most kids learn and love to sing the ABC song. Build on that pleasure by pointing to each letter as you teach the song. This one activity alone (repeated many times) will give your child a huge advantage once he enters school.

Toys. Try to avoid toys that simply entertain and provide no opportunity for real learning. An example of the no-learning toy is one that allows the child to push a button or pull a string, and then watch to see what happens. Strive to get toys and games that necessitate your child's involvement as opposed to observation. Here are a few "quick and dirty" questions to ask yourself when you are contemplating a toy purchase.

- Does it provide an opportunity for creativity or imagination?

- Will it aid the memory process?

- Does it give practice in seeing or hearing differences?

- Does it provide an opportunity to use the small muscles that later will be used when writing?

- Does it require the child's interaction?

If the answer to any of these questions is "Yes", get your billfold out.

All of us occasionally allow ourselves to be suckered into buying the latest fad toy or junk item for our child or grandchild. When that happens, don't beat yourself up. Simply remind yourself to be more discerning the next time. Hey, we don't have to be perfect in order to do a good parenting or grand-parenting job. All we have to do is give it our best shot.

There is a Jewish proverb that says, "One mother teaches more than a hundred teachers." You, the parent, are your child's first teacher and his best teacher. It's an awesome responsibility, but one that brings immeasurable rewards. Good luck!

The richest person on the planet can buy nothing that equals the value of an hour spent with a child.
                                        –The Author

3

IS HE READY?

Although the cutoff dates for entering kindergarten vary somewhat throughout our fifty states, one thing remains constant. A large majority of conscientious parents of five year olds (or soon to be five) wonder if their kids are really ready for such a momentous step.

For the past 25 years parents have worried about whether or not their five year old is ready for kindergarten. (Prior to that, they simply sent him to school in the fall following his fifth birthday – no ifs, ands, or buts about it.) But, we know so much more about child development today than we did thirty years ago. And, as in almost all areas of life, more knowledge means more decisions. (It doesn't seem fair, does it?)

In the "olden days", kindergarten was almost always the child's first school experience, and its focus was on the child's social adjustment to school. Kindergarten was usually a half-day program. The curriculum and activities were separate from the rest of the school and the purpose was to prepare the child for first grade and "real" learning.

Today, 62% of American schools have instituted a full day kindergarten program. Many other districts are attempting to find additional funding to use for that purpose. Regardless of whether a district's kindergarten is half or full day, the program has become an integral part of the primary school's curriculum. The focus has shifted from being primarily social, to one that is both social and academic. Because of this shift, parents often feel a need to determine if their child is ready for kindergarten, or if a different one-year option would be in his best interest.

Although there are no hard and fast rules to determine a child's readiness for kindergarten, there are numerous guidelines to consider. I'd like to share some of these with you in the hope that they might assist you in making the best decision for your child's fifth year of life.

Does your child...
- Recognize and name colors
- Sort items by color and shape
- Understand and use words such as *in, out, under, over,*
- Know his body parts (not *those* body parts) – I'm referring to head, neck, knee, etc.)
- Include a head, body, arms and legs in his drawing of a person

Does your child...
- Put puzzles together
- Cut with scissors
- Attempt to tie his shoes
- Hold a pencil, crayon, or marker
- Ride any three-wheeled "vehicle"
- Bounce a ball

Does your child...
- Arrange items in a group according to size, shape and color
- Use words like bigger, smaller, more, less, fewer...

- Count from four to ten *objects* (remember, this is far more difficult than simply *saying* the numbers from 1 to 10)

Does your child...
- Talk in sentences
- Sing or say nursery rhymes
- Pretend to read
- Tell fantasy stories as though they are true
- Ask "why" and "how" questions (now stop groaning – that's how kids learn)

Does your child...
- Enjoy being read to
- Look at books on his own
- Recognize his own name in print
- Recognize familiar print such as Pizza Hut, Wal Mart, Toys R Us, and McDonalds

Please keep in mind that just because your little one may not have reached all of the mileposts yet, he is not necessarily doomed to "failure." ALL KIDS DEVELOP AT DIFFERENT RATES AND AT DIFFERENT STAGES. When kids come to school already knowing how to interact with others, how to follow routines, and how to listen to and follow directions, they are basically ready to start in with the academic development. If your child is adept in these areas, he most likely will pick up rather quickly any readiness skills that he may have missed along the way.

Occasionally a parent allows circumstances unrelated to the child's readiness determine his decision regarding kindergarten enrollment. I have heard (many times) reasons such as closeness of birthday to enrollment cutoff date, size of child, grandparents' expectations, and not "falling behind" same-age neighbors or cousins. And by far the most frequent reason (but not always verbalized) is the one tied to the vision of eliminating some childcare expense. All reasons are understandable, and some have merit. We'll discuss each briefly.

When in doubt about kindergarten enrollment, the child's birth date and size can both play a legitimate part in the decision making process. There are a few generalizations that you may want to consider.

- Boys mature later than girls. If a boy turns five anytime within three months prior to the kindergarten cutoff date, seriously consider an option other than regular kindergarten.

- A particularly small child may lag slightly behind in learning, and can often profit from a one-year program other than traditional kindergarten. Conversely, an unusually large child (either height or weight) might feel "different" and out-of-place if held out of school an extra year. The exceptionally large child is often served best by entering kindergarten at age five.

- Early childhood development (birth to age 3) is closely tied to school readiness. If a child has been late to sit, crawl, walk, and talk, he is perhaps a "late bloomer." He will probably do best if he enters kindergarten at age six. Of course the opposite is true for the infant/toddler who has met all milestones at, or before the expected age.

Grandparent expectations ("He's five years old and should be in kindergarten") are irrelevant and should not be a part of the decision-making process. End of discussion. (Remember, I'm a grandma too.)

It is totally understandable why parents hesitate to hold their child out of kindergarten for an extra year when their same-age cousins or playmates will be trudging off to school in the fall. Parents don't want their little one to feel "left out" or lose his playmates. When this situation occurs, parents need to put on their farsighted glasses. That is, they need to determine which choice will be the most beneficial over the long haul. Sometimes it is not the easiest choice, nor the one that makes everyone happy at the time.

I've saved the "biggie" for last. MONEY! Many parents have struggled for five years to pay the cost of adequate childcare and they are ready to eliminate that expenditure *now*. And who can blame them? Not I. (I worked before, and all during my boys' growing up years. I can still feel the pinch of writing out those checks for – in my case – a sitter to come to the home.) But once more, pick up those glasses we just talked about. One more year of stretching a tight budget is really a small price to pay for something that can realistically affect your child's entire life.

You may think I'm getting a bit melodramatic when I say that an extra year at home "can affect a child's entire life." But, hear me out on this one. A child learns to love (or hate) school in kindergarten and first grade. During that time he forms attitudes about his own value as a person and his worth as a learner. Those attitudes will accompany him all the way through school and into adulthood. If he feels good about himself as a learner, he will continue to soar higher and enjoy the flight. If he constantly has to struggle to keep from "being held back", he will think of his educational trip as a painful, never ending journey.

An extra year at home for the "not-quite-ready" five year old does not insure a wonderful academic experience, but it certainly makes the odds a whole lot better. If you're in doubt, I suggest that you err on the side of caution. The chances are minute that you will cause any harm if you choose to keep your child out of a traditional kindergarten for one year. If you compare that to the damage that will occur if you send him to school before he is ready, the decision is a no-brainer.

If you have looked at every angle and still have reservations about your little one's readiness for school, I suggest you discuss the situation with an experienced and respected kindergarten teacher employed in your district. She has "walked the walk" and will be happy to "talk the talk" with you. After all, five and six year-olds are her business. She is the expert. And what's more, she'll offer her opinion for free!

You know that the beginning is the most important part of any work, especially in the case of a young and tender thing; for that is the time at which character is being formed.

- Plato

4

NICKING THE TIES

In this chapter we will look at the importance of nicking (not severing) the apron strings at an early age. I will explain why it is important to begin early to gradually decrease the young child's dependency on the parent. I will also offer some suggestions on how to accomplish this task.

For the benefit of you young readers, the apron was an article of clothing used in the olden days to cover the "housedress." An apron was worn in an attempt to keep the dress from getting soiled while butchering chickens, slopping hogs, and mopping floors. (I wonder why anyone would call those "the good old days?") Anyway, senior citizens (even more "senior" than I) tell me that if a stranger appeared at the door, small children would hide behind their mother and cling to her apron strings. Thus the saying, "It's time to cut the apron strings."

This chapter is about the day-to-day routines that face all five to eight year old kids. Please do not let me confuse you. I am not suggesting that you initiate these suggestions on the first day of kindergarten when you woefully say good-bye to your "baby." On that momentous occasion you are entitled to feel like the bottom has dropped out of your world. Of course you are almost blinded by tears - tears that cause you to consider requesting a police escort to help you drive back home safely. Those reactions are normal and natural. They go along with parenting. You brought this child into the world. You've invested more than five years in this little one's life. You deserve to immerse yourself with some nostalgic recollections and shed a few tears. You've worked hard to earn your invitation to this pity party, and you need not apologize to anyone. So there!

But, when those first days of kindergarten are in the past, it's time to start nicking away at those apron strings. Why so soon, you ask? Because, you are preparing him for real life.

Just as a house needs a foundation in order to stand firm, so does a person. And when do we build the foundation? We start at the beginning. When we apply this to developing a child's independence, it means we start when he enters kindergarten.

As your child grows older you will want to gradually, but consistently, help him to diminish his dependence on you as he relies more and more on himself. Your goal is to have him be somewhat self-sufficient and independent by the time he graduates from high school. Yes, he will always need (and deserve) your emotional support. He might even want your financial support. But, putting those issues aside, he will be much better equipped to face the **real** world if you have given him the gift of guided independence.

As a young adult he will get to work or class on time. She will remember to fulfill all of her job duties or study assignments before calling it quits for the day (or heading out to party). He will be able to adjust his expenditures to his income. She will accept (albeit grudgingly) constructive criticism from her boss or instructor. He will not rely on defense mechanisms like, "My dad's going to sue you!" She will usually obey the laws of society. And if she "forgets" and gets caught, she'll know that she has only herself to blame. She will also understand that she, and no one else, will have to pay the consequences.

The bottom line is this. Your child will be better prepared to tackle the bumps on the road of life if he has been given the gift of guided independence. And if at some point he encounters a mountain, he'll have the equipment and the experience to climb that mountain.

Here are a few suggestions that may help you as you begin the task of steering your child toward independence.

After the first few days of kindergarten, encourage your child to enter the school building and proceed to the classroom by himself. This may need to be a gradual process. (Remember, new tasks can be pretty scary – even for us adults.) Begin by walking with her into the classroom for the first week. Walk with her *to* the classroom door the second week. Walk with her *to* the front entrance of the school building on the third week. Thereafter, give her a kiss and a wave goodbye as she departs from your car or leaves the house for the bus. (This plan may need to be modified in order to insure safety precautions for your particular community or neighborhood.)

You may have noticed in the preceding paragraph that I used the word "walk." I chose that word intentionally with no intention of using it as an admonition against running. Instead, I am suggesting that you do not carry your school-age child in your arms to and from the building. He needs to be seeing himself as "growing up", and grown-ups aren't carried in arms. (Forget the honeymoon-threshold scenario.)

Make the "tote-bag patrol" a joint duty divided between your child and at least one adult. It is preferable if that adult is a parent, but if your particular circumstances make that impossible, a babysitter or a grandparent can assume that responsibility.

Go through the tote bag every night and prepare it for the following day. Preparation might simply mean emptying the bag. However, it might also involve returning a book that is due or providing some requested materials for an upcoming school project. It might mean responding to a teacher's question with a note or telephone call.

If there are notations from the teacher on any of your child's papers, read them and discuss them with your little one. If there are papers that indicate a troublesome area, work with your child in an attempt to clear up misconceptions or missing skills. And above all else, look for something in your child's work to praise – EVERY SINGLE DAY.

When the bag is ready to go, have your child place it by the front door or in some other predetermined location so that it can easily found and ready to go in the morning.

Depending on the season, instruct your child to put any outerwear that he might need with his tote-bag before he goes to bed. Few things are more frustrating to both parent and child than running through the house at the last minute in the morning hunting for boots, mittens, or even shoes. The parent ends up driving to work as a prime candidate for road rage. The kid (who incidentally has managed to avoid accepting responsibility for his own welfare) heads for school with one nasty attitude. Nobody wins!

Seriously question the necessity (or the wisdom) of taking forgotten items to school just to bail Junior out of trouble. Perhaps a question you may want to ask yourself is this one. "Will the absence of this item really affect his well being, or will it simply create a bump in the road?" Let your answer determine your action. (Bumps aren't fatal.)

Be certain your child knows when he leaves for school where he is to go at the end of the day and how he is to get there. Not knowing for sure who will be picking him up or where he is to go, causes a child excessive and unnecessary worry. That kind of fretting affects his entire day and prevents maximum learning. It also creates a dependence on the teacher or school secretary to solve a problem that the child didn't create, and shouldn't be facing.

It is particularly important for the young child to know what to do in case of an unexpected early dismissal due to weather conditions or some other type of emergency. Armed with the knowledge of where he should go and how he should get there gives the child a feeling of independency. He is in his little mind, "master of his own destiny." HE IS GROWING UP!

I would like to end this chapter with a note of caution that is probably obvious to all who are reading it. But, just in case...guiding your child toward independence is totally different than pushing him out the door to make his own mistakes and "paddle his own canoe." That mindset is synonymous with neglect and could justifiably be called abuse. I would *never* endorse or condone that type of parenting. And more importantly - neither would you!

There are only two lasting bequests we can hope to give our children. One of these is roots, the other, wings.
-Hodding Carter

5

GOODBYE, GUILT

Statistics vary a bit, but roughly 80% of our school-age kids have moms who work outside the home. I know of no way to scientifically measure the percentage of working moms who try to support their child's educational efforts while they simultaneously hold down a job. However, my experience of working with hundreds of parents leads me to believe that the biggest majority of working mothers do have this goal. I strongly feel they have exactly the same desires for their children as stay-at-home moms do. They simply have less time available with which to achieve their goals.

In this chapter I will offer some suggestions on how moms working outside the home can manage to support the educational efforts of their children, and simultaneously say goodbye to their guilt. Perhaps there will be a tip or two that might also be helpful to mothers who have chosen to stay home during their child's academic years. Although this chapter is addressed to moms, it is equally applicable to the single-parent fathers who are heading a household and stay-at-home dads. (I guess you could call it an "equal-opportunity" chapter.)

Go through the tote bag or backpack EVERY night. Although I referred to this task in the last chapter, I would like to expand on the topic because of its importance. I believe that *carefully going through the tote bag or backpack on a nightly basis is the single most important thing a mom can do to support her child's educational endeavors*. The contents of the bag provide information that is extremely valuable. When the materials contained in the bag are carefully and regularly examined, mom is aware of what is taking place at school. She is also alerted early on to any problems that may be developing.

Student-completed work can often be found in the bag. The frequency will depend on teacher policy and grade level. If the bag is "inspected" on a nightly basis, mom will always be up to date on what her child is doing in school, and how well he is doing it.

Moms should make a concerted effort to say something good about every paper or project in the bag. It can be as simple as, "I'm glad you remembered to write your name." Teachers are taught in methods' classes to begin every parent-teacher conference with a positive statement about the student before launching into a list of negatives. I believe this is also good advice for the mother who is examining her child's work. A tower must be built up, before it can be knocked down.

When there is work that indicates confusion or lack of understanding, it should be discussed with the student. Many times a mother's fifteen minutes of one-on-one time can clear up a simple misconception. A teacher working with a classroom of twenty-five can temporarily miss the "gray area" of one. This is particularly true when it involves a very shy child who is hesitant (or refuses) to request help. Unfortunately, the wheel that doesn't squeak often misses the oil.

When a student is beyond the primary grades, a mother may feel uncomfortable about giving guidance that targets a skill deficiency. This situation is universal and is NOT a cause for guilt. Terminology changes. Methods change. Understandably, parents don't want to confuse their child by teaching them the "wrong" way. Besides that, we adults tend to forget much of what we learned in school if we aren't utilizing that information on a regular basis. (Did I hear you say you don't remember what a conjunctive phrase is, or how to find the square root of 6,884? Neither do I!) However, a parent's feeling of inadequacy (although typical and normal) is not a permission slip to ignore an academic problem that surfaces with an older child.

The mother of an older child who notices an academic deficiency or lack of understanding should immediately contact the teacher and ask for advice. She should not wait for a school-scheduled conference to see if the problem will "work itself out."

The teacher might explain how mom can help, or she might suggest a time when she herself can work individually with the child. She might arrange for an older in-school student tutor to provide assistance. Or, she might offer some names of tutors-for-hire that could be of help.

The bottom line is this. When mom contacts teacher with a concern, the teacher becomes more aware of the student's problem. She also is made mindful of mom's desire to have the problem addressed. The child sees mom is not ignoring the problem, and is determined to find help. It's a win-win combination.

The tote or book bag may also include a note requesting one or more items for a particular school project coming up (sometimes the following day). That type of request needs to be addressed in a timely fashion. If it is not, the child is forced to inform the teacher that he cannot participate in the special activity because he doesn't have the necessary materials. Invariably the teacher will make some type of arrangement to avoid excluding the child, but – make no mistake about it - damage will have been done. The child will have been made to feel "different" through his acceptance of an altered requirement.

Occasionally the bag might contain a personal note from the teacher regarding an academic or behavioral concern. When that occurs, mom is obliged to acknowledge the communication immediately. That can be in the form of a telephone call (on break time) or a note. The important aspect is that once again, teacher knows mom is on top of things and is willing to help.

And here's a little secret. When a teacher has mom's attention and is assured of her cooperation, that teacher is going to work doubly hard to try to correct any problem that may be surfacing. Why? I'm not sure, but I think it goes along with the quote that says, "A problem shared leaves half-a-problem."

On rare occasions the bag might contain a student-congratulatory message from the teacher or principal. When that momentous event happens, MAKE THE MOST OF IT. Mount it on the refrigerator, call Grandma, or go out for pizza. (I suggest you avoid toy or money rewards. They set an expensive, unnecessary precedent.) The child's real reward is in seeing his parents' pride.

Often the bag will contain some form of general information from the teacher or principal. Although both of these groups tend to get carried away with Microsoft Word, (I was constantly guilty of that "crime") they are writing a message they feel is important. Granted, a working-outside-the-home mom is tired and frazzled at the end of the day. But, she still needs to take the time to read communication that comes from the school. It may regard school policy. It might be about a child-health issue, or it might be a parenting tip. At any rate, someone connected with the school felt that it was worth his time to write it, and the taxpayer's money to send it.

If for no other reason, mom should read all school communication so she will not feel foolish when she calls the school with a question that has already been addressed and sent home via the tote bag.

A daily tote or book bag check demonstrates to the child his mom's interest and involvement in his school life. When the checkup is done in a nurturing and positive manner, the rewards are innumerable.

Handle homework with consistency. Because practice/drill for the young child and homework for the older child is such a huge area, it deserves its own chapter. However, it *is* an area that a working mom can and should address so we will look at the bare basics at this time. You will want (I hope) to read Chapter 21 for a more in-depth discussion.

Naturally the "rules" for practice/drill (K-2) or student homework (3-12) are different due to age and maturity. We'll start with some basic guidelines for working with the primary age youngster.

It is extremely important to keep work sessions short. A fifteen-minute session once each evening is far more beneficial than one two-hour session on the weekend. More damage is done and fewer benefits are gained when practice periods are too long. The child tires and looses interest. The parent tires and becomes angry. Everybody looses. Nobody wins.

Every attempt should be made to keep the practice/drill session fun and positive. Mom needs to remember that honey catches more flies than vinegar does. A child cannot learn when he is the object of angry words, "subtle" gestures, or verbal threats.

An adult's unsuccessful attempt to teach a child something that appears exceptionally simple is **extremely** frustrating. If mom begins to feel her tolerance level has reached the breaking point, she should stop the session - immediately. She might simply say that she is tired (no lie), and suggest they work on it another time.

Homework for the older child becomes a stickier situation for a variety of reasons. He is expected to do his homework independently. He is expected to understand, without asking, that mom or dad will not to do his homework for him. He is more involved in extra-curricular activities. He may hold down a job. He may have found "the love of his life." It all comes down to the undeniable fact that he is older, and he exercises more will power. The other part of the picture is that mom is still the parent, and MOM KNOWS BEST!

At this point we'll look only briefly at some ways the working mom can address the homework issue with her older child. (Don't forget about Chapter 21).

Mom should work with her older child to develop a mutually acceptable time for the homework period, and then enforce compliance. If no time is agreeable with the student – too bad, how sad. Mom needs to exercise her rights and responsibilities as a parent and insist that compliance is not an option for debate. The timeframe is the only part of the equation that is negotiable. The older student should be allowed to work around his social desires and extra-curricular activities within reason. Once a time is mutually agreed upon, it is a parent's responsibility to see that it is consistently adhered to. Failure to comply should be met with consequences appropriate to the age of the child.

Are any of these suggestions easy? Oh, no. Can they really be carried through in today's society? Oh, yes. Mother won't get any "You're the Best Mom in the World" trophy from her kid, but she will have the satisfaction of knowing that she chose the wisest – albeit the most difficult - course of action. (The trophy will come later in the form of a diploma.)

Demand they eat something for breakfast. I realize that some kids absolutely hate a traditional breakfast. Even the thought of a scrambled egg and a piece of toast can send some kids running to the bathroom. If that's the case, Mom needs to compromise. Let Little Miss Touchy Stomach chow down a piece of last night's leftover pizza, or even a slice of gooey chocolate cake. Okay, I hear you. Nutritionists, dieticians, and school cooks are ready to clobber me with a spatula. People in the medical field want to head my direction with a scalpel. But hey, something in the tummy is better than nothing. A youngster with a totally empty stomach simply cannot learn as well as the child who has eaten breakfast.

What about the mom who goes to work before it's time for the child's breakfast? No problem. Today most schools across the country provide a tasty and healthy breakfast menu on every school day. And as Mr. Food says, "It is s-o-o-o good." Like lunch, breakfasts are available at free and reduced rates for those who qualify. The working mom should take advantage of this "perk", and offer apologies to no one. (She might use that extra twenty minutes to treat herself to a cup of coffee and a glance at the newspaper. She deserves it!)

Gather at the table as a family for the evening meal. By "the family", I simply mean those living in the household. That might mean two people, or eight. The number doesn't matter. What does matter is the table, with the TV turned OFF. Why? It provides an excellent opportunity to share the day's events. That means mom tells something about her day and requests some information about her child's day. Hint: Unless she wants to hear, "nuthin", she should ask her child to tell about the best part of his day, instead of the traditional, "What did you do in school today?" She very possibly might hear the "worst" part of his day too. And that's okay. It provides insight as to what is really going on in the child's school life.

Insist on a healthy bedtime on school nights. Of course, individual children have different sleep requirements, but as a rule, primary age children should be asleep by 9 p.m. Children beyond age ten can normally handle a 10 o'clock bedtime.

Parents of teenagers need to ignore all bargaining attempts, and insist that school night bedtime be no later than eleven o'clock. (They needn't buy into the, "I have to study" ploy. An appropriate response to that is, "Sorry, but you need to plan your day better. Goodnight!") If a parent is consistent with a rule and avoids exceptions, the kid will eventually give in – even a teenager.

I strongly encourage parents to spend the last fifteen to twenty minutes before bedtime promoting some kind of reading activity. The small child should be allowed to choose a book and the way he wants it shared. He may choose to sit on mom's lap or have dad sit next to his bed. When he learns to read, he may want to do the reading while a parent listens. The older child might simply choose to retreat to his room for some private-all-alone reading. (You may want to check your supply of stashed-away Playboy and Playgirl magazines). Any method at all is perfectly fine, as long as it is a relaxing, healthy way to end the day.

I'd like to close this chapter with a little "pep talk." Whether you are a 'working' mom, or a 'stay-at-home' mom, don't beat yourself up about your decision! Frankly, I get sick and tired of reading articles that uphold one choice and condemn the other. You, and you alone, know what is best for your family situation. Whether you choose (or are required) to work outside the home does not affect your ability to support your child's educational endeavors one iota. It's how you use the time available that counts!

One mother teaches more than a hundred teachers.
-Jewish Proverb

6

LET'S TALK

There is no school-related event that elicits the widely divergent range of emotions like that of the parent-teacher conference. It all begins when the scheduled appointment notification first meets the parent's eye.

Some parents wait with eager anticipation to hear how their child is progressing academically and socially in the classroom. These are the parents who already know their child is doing well. They have looked at the school papers bearing happy faces and positive comments. They have listened eagerly each night as their child reported on the events of the school day. And finally, they have dealt with the struggle of keeping their child in the house in the morning long enough to guarantee he won't arrive at school before the custodian. Their child loves school. The conference will only confirm what they already know. Life is good. They can hardly wait!

Other parents experience emotions that range from wariness to absolute dread. They also have looked at the papers that have come home from school. They have listened with disappointment as their child responded "Nuthin'" to the routine question, "What did you do in school today?" And they too have struggled with the morning routine, but for a different reason. Their child doesn't want to leave the comfort of bed or home. And besides, except for their kindergartener, these parents have heard it all before! They wish their scheduled conference were over and done with!

First, let me assure you that both reactions, as well as everything in between, are perfectly normal and understandable. Throughout my teaching career I sat on the teacher's side of the desk approximately 3,780 times. During that time I also sat on the parents' side of the desk 78 times. Contrary to what either of my two sons might say, the parents' side was not always equivalent to champagne and candlelight. It is not just a meaningless cliché when I say, "I know how you feel."

Ironically, the parent isn't the only one that experiences apprehension about an upcoming conference. The child worries about what infraction or deficiency the teacher will relate to his parents. The teacher struggles with doubt regarding her ability to present each student's strengths and weaknesses in a positive, non-offensive manner. Yes, conference time can be, and often is, stressful for all involved. It is, however, extremely important and should *never* be intentionally avoided.

All parents like to hear good things about their kids. It makes them proud, and they think it reflects well on them as parents. Teachers are no different. A happy, successful student makes the teacher proud, and she thinks it reflects well on her ability to teach.

But how do teachers relay and parents receive news when it involves an academically, socially, emotionally, or behaviorally struggling student? Not so good, I'm afraid.

Naturally, the parent is worried and disappointed. Sometimes he suffers pangs of guilt because he thinks his child's problems reflect negatively on his parenting skills or genetic makeup. He mighty cry, respond in a defensive manner, or even stand up and head for the door. (I saw all of these reactions during my teaching career, and they were always heartbreaking!)

Perhaps surprisingly, the teacher of a struggling student understands this type of parental reaction because she too feels the pain of worry and guilt. When a student struggles or fails in any area, the teacher always has doubts about her own competency. She wonders what, if anything, she could or should be doing differently in order to reach that child.

The REAL purpose for the parent-teacher conference is to provide an opportunity where parents and teachers can share information and work together. It is designed to help determine the best possible way to meet the unique needs of each individual student. Parents and teachers need to avoid the tendency to assign blame, or wallow in guilt. Both are negative responses that do nothing positive to help the child.

I believe that we need to approach the parent-teacher conference as a visit between partners who share a common interest. Neither partner should consider it as a lecture where the teacher speaks, and the parent sits and listens. True, the teacher knows how the child performs in the classroom and how he relates to others. And true, it is the teacher's obligation to share that information with parents.

Often, however, the teacher does not know the cause of a child's problem. That is where the parent comes in. Nobody knows a child as well as the parent does. It is the parent's ethical and moral obligation to share any information that might help the teacher to better understand his child's problems or deficiencies. It is also the parent's duty to offer any suggestions he might have that could possibly increase the chances for his child's success in school. The child's teacher wants parental input, and she needs it. She understands and empathizes with the fact that some parents are reluctant to attend, but she needs their assistance.

Parents should understand that the teacher also has some apprehensions to deal with. She doesn't enjoy sharing the less than stellar observations she may have noticed in a child, but it is her duty to do so. Perhaps we all need to remember that parents and teachers are not adversaries. They are partners working toward the same goal. And as in all partnerships, each member needs to contribute and carry his share of the load.

The word "partnership" brings to mind another conference issue that pertains to roughly half of the students in our schools. I am speaking of the parents who are divorced, separated, or otherwise estranged. There is no one pat "rule" that fits every situation, but there are a few guidelines that I hope will be beneficial.

IF both natural parents can be in a small confined area for 20 minutes and refrain from arguing or assigning blame, that is the preferable scenario. Both get to hear the same information and each has the opportunity to contribute. For obvious reasons, it is best to leave the stepparent or "significant other" at home when both natural parents attend a conference simultaneously.

In some cases, divorced or estranged parents attending the conference together simply won't work due to unresolved hostilities. The solution to that situation is really quite simple. All the non-custodial parent need do is call the office at his child's attendance center and request a separate conference time. The teacher will be eager to visit with the non-custodial parent, to answer any questions he (or she) might have, and to consider thoughtfully any suggestions that parent might offer. Teachers understand that both parents are interested in their child, and therefore they want input from both.

Before leaving this topic, I have one more suggestion for BOTH parents of a disintegrated relationship. The parent-teacher conference is not an appropriate time to assign blame or to seek information about an ex-partner. The teacher ethically cannot respond to negative statements or questions involving anyone other than the student for whom the conference is being held. In short, both parents of a disintegrated relationship need to remember that they are attending the conference to discuss the welfare of their child, and nothing else.

I would like to conclude this chapter with some questions. Why is it that we eagerly attend all of our older child's athletic, music, and drama events, but we barely even consider attending his conference? Is it a matter of what's important and what is not? Do we enjoy watching our kid more than hearing about his academic achievements or deficiencies? Or have we simply "given up the ship" with an attitude of helplessness? Although all of these reasons may play a part, I suspect the last is perhaps the most prevalent.

If you are one of many who do not attend conferences once your child leaves the elementary building, I would ask you to reconsider. Your child needs to see where your priorities are. For as long as you live, your child is going to need your guidance and your direction. Don't let him down through your own feelings of helplessness. Show him that you will *never* give up on him. Go to that older kid's conference!

It is probably not love that makes the world go around, but rather those mutually supportive alliances through which partners recognize their dependence on each other for the achievement of shared and private goals.

- Fred A. Allen

7

GET A "SUB"

Some of the first words a toddler speaks are, "Watch me." He wants a parent to watch him run, climb a tree, or wiggle his nose. He wants to show how he can make his soda bubble while blowing through a straw, or flaunt the beautiful sand sculpture he has just fashioned. This is an inborn and universal trait of all kids.

Every child wants to demonstrate his accomplishments to the most important people in his life. He is certainly not consciously aware of any "motive", but he has one. He is seeking an affirmation of his worth. He wants to hear that he is special and to be told once again that his parents are *very* proud of him. What's more, he needs to hear these words of acceptance again and again in order to become all that he can be. It's a non-negotiable responsibility of a parent to give attention and to offer praise whenever possible.

Realistically, it is not always possible to watch our child "perform" once he ventures off to school. Every parent I've ever known wants to attend all activities and programs in which his child appears. However, there are times when it simply isn't possible to do so. It might be a work schedule that interferes (I don't know why employers insist we show up), a sick child at home, an ailing parent in need of assistance, or personal illness. Or perhaps the director (or teacher) didn't give enough advance notice!

Many years ago I made that error. My first grade class had been engaged for a solid week in a mini-unit built around the classic tale of the Three Little Pigs. Several of the children had brought their own versions from home, and we read them all. We compared vocabulary, style, and illustrations. We made lists of likenesses and differences. We discussed possible reasons for the various endings to the story. We voted on which version we liked best. (Of course each kid voted for the version he had contributed.) We made miniature houses from straw, sticks, and Styrofoam bricks. We ate, drank, and slept with those little porkers. The kids loved it. As a culminating activity (I thought we needed to move on), I divided the class into three groups and told them they could have one hour to plan and practice their own dramatization. Each group could act out the play any way they wished, as long as every member had a part. For bribery (yes, teachers do resort to that occasionally) I told them if they worked cooperatively and kept the noise level to a tolerable degree, we would invite the other four first grades in the building to come and watch our productions.

Although the noise level was somewhat questionable, they did work together and there were no tears, cuts or bruises. As requested, our invited guests came at 1 o'clock and watched intently as Room 2 acted out their plays. The attendees were a wonderful audience. They gave my little actors and actresses hearty applause and a number of high fives. It was a superb way to end the unit. Or more accurately, it was intended to be the end.

Before I could see the hind pocket of the last guest leaving the room, Jimmy yelled out, "Let's invite our parents to come see our play." The entire class began to cheer. Oh my, that wasn't in my long-range lesson plan. But, I decided to give in and honor their request.

Although I understood the kids' desire to have their parents see the play, I didn't feel we should utilize any more time in practicing and polishing. Consequently, I hastily typed a note to the parents and invited them to come the *following day* for Room 2's multiple productions of THE THREE LITTLE PIGS. (I explained in the note how this was an impromptu activity, and they should not expect perfection.)

The following morning, most of my little cherubs were waiting for me at the front door of the school. They were s-o-o excited. I decided to dispense with the usual before-school activities of checking books in, sharpening pencils, etc., and assigned each group to an area where they could practice their play one last time. It was then I noticed that "Susie" was absent.

I remember thinking it was odd for Susie to miss school. She hadn't been absent (or tardy) one time the entire year. I simply couldn't imagine what might cause her to miss this special event. After all, she had been chosen by her production mates to be the BIG BAD WOLF – the most coveted character in the cast.

As I was contemplating the various reasons that might account for Susie's absence, she walked in the door. Her eyes were red and puffy, and she was clutching a very soggy Kleenex. Fearing the worst, I walked quickly to her and bent down to ask what was wrong. With that simple gesture of concern, she started (actually, she resumed) crying - uncontrollably. Between sobs she said, "My mom can't come to my play because she works out of town and she didn't have enough notice to make different arrangements. And my dad can't come 'cause he owns a store and some customers might come in."

Did you ever think you were doing something good, only to learn later that your action had caused someone pain? That was my experience that day, and I have never forgotten it. But, I did learn from it. As a teacher, I learned that I needed to give longer notice when I was inviting parents to come to school to watch their child perform. As a parent, I learned that when an unavoidable situation made it impossible for me to attend a school or extra-curricular event, I needed to GET A SUBSTITUTE.

It is important for you to understand that I am not talking about enlisting the help of a substitute parent so that you can play a round of golf, "do" lunch, or go fishing. Those activities are optional and should always take second place to your child's needs. I am referring to the times when you have a perfectly legitimate and unavoidable reason for not attending an event that showcases your child's accomplishments. The times when you desperately want to attend, but absolutely cannot.

You are heartsick because you know your child will be scanning and searching the audience for your face. He will be hoping against hope that some last minute miracle will have made it possible for you to appear. How do you know this? Because you've seen it before! You remember how, when he finally spots you, his expression changes instantly. His worried frown turns into a smile that seems to stretch all the way from school to home. He is reassured. He is at ease. Someone who loves him very much is there to watch him, to enjoy him, and when it's all over – to praise him. It is the same special someone who will ultimately give him a hug, and return him to the safety and comfort of his home.

The little kid will wave his arm off just to make sure you see him among the crowd. (What, see him? He's the only kid on the stage, isn't he?) The big kid is much too "cool" for arm waving. As a matter of fact, you might not get so much as a smile from your older dude. But make no mistake about it. He is aware you are there, and he is mighty glad of it. The big kid wants and needs your presence just as much as the little kid does. Big kids just don't show it!

Yes, you understand all of this, but you still can't make it this one time. So what do you do? Lift your chin up, and read on. My plan for soliciting the help of a substitute parent will help both you and your child. It will allow you to stop kicking yourself in the backside because you will have made lemonade out of lemons! It will help your child to understand that an alternative course of action can be both fulfilling and rewarding. And ultimately, it will help both you and your offspring deal with disappointment.

The timetable for my suggestions will vary, depending on whether your reason for missing an event is known ahead of time, or is due to an emergency.

As soon as you are aware of an event conflict, sit down one on one with your child and explain exactly why you will be unable to attend. Next, suggest two or three names (grandma, next-door neighbor, babysitter, older sibling, etc.) that you know would love to attend just to watch him. Then ask your child to choose the substitute *he* would like to invite.

If time permits, take your child with you and go to the chosen person's home and make a big deal of the "invitation." Discuss with the "sub", the approximate area where she (or he) plans to sit, and make your child aware of that location. Be absolutely certain your little one knows precisely where and how he will connect with his substitute parent following the performance. If your child's special "guest of honor" is able to drive him either to or from the event, so much the better. In any case, your child should be informed about the transportation details (if there are any) well in advance of the "performance."

During the time between the invitation and the event, make a big deal about how excited and honored the substitute is feeling. It's also a great opportunity to convey to your child how fortunate your family is to have that special person in your lives.

Within a few days following the event, assist your child in buying an appropriate card of Thanks to send to his "special someone." Encourage her to write (or copy) as much of the note as possible in her own handwriting. It is also appropriate and desirable for you to include a few words that express your own sentiments of gratitude.

A plan along these lines (with variations for time, circumstances, and age of the child) can accomplish so much with so little effort. Your guilt feelings will vanish. Your child's disappointment at your absence will be drastically reduced. And best of all, you will have helped to strengthen what was probably already an emotional bond between your child and his special guest.

I have one final suggestion for all of you lucky people who are able to attend your child's programs, plays, contests, or concerts. Please set a good example for kids by demonstrating the kind of good old-fashioned "attendance behavior" that you would like your kids to display when they become parents.

If you are attending a concert, a play, or some similar event, do not talk (or even whisper) while students are performing. If the event is some type of contest, do not yell caustic remarks to your child, to his competitor, or to the officials. (Delay your advice until later. The coach can handle the on-site instruction.) Acknowledge the fact that every kid is trying to do his best. And please remember - "winning" isn't

the most important part of a contest. Effort and attitude is.
When we focus on the most important aspects of any
competitive activity involving kids, there are no losers. They
are all winners, and they deserve to be treated as such.

At the risk of sounding simplistic, I suggest that it will
serve our kids favorably if we enact the Golden Rule when we
attend functions that involve kids competing against each
other. That is, we need to treat other people's children the
same way we want our kids to be treated by others. Kids
model what they *see* more quickly and more effectively than
what they hear. We need to ban together and show them how
to conduct themselves at a public event. We'll be doing our
kids a favor, and society too.

*Each difficult moment has the potential to open my eyes
and open my heart.*

- Myla Kabat-Zinn

8

THE "B" WORD

My former students would probably attest to the fact that few things tried Mrs. McTaggart's patience as much as did the statement, "This is boring!" As I reflect back on my many years in the classroom, I can't help but feel a little sorry for the kid who was the first one to utter those words in any given school year. (It was rare to have any child repeat the phrase after hearing my "sermon.")

The sermon went something like this. "Nobody is BORED in my classroom. I work hard to plan fun and interesting activities that will allow you to learn. When you finish your work earlier than others, there are many choices of quiet things to do. There are baskets full of good books to choose from. You may also use the computers, the writing center, the art center, or the manipulative math corner. Now please, do NOT let me hear the word "bored" again!" Amen.

I have little doubt that the year's unlucky first offender heard my speech and had thoughts similar to those of Calvin (Hobbes's buddy) as portrayed in one of my favorite comic strips. In the first two frames, Calvin is sitting at his school desk saying nothing. He appears to be as animated as one might be if he were watching paint dry. In the third frame Calvin screams, "BORRRING!" The final frame shows Calvin heading for the Principal's office muttering, "Yeah, yeah...kill the messenger." Although not many kids made the mistake of verbally uttering the "B" word a second time (at least in my earshot), I suspect they said it in their minds over and over again.

Contrary to popular opinion, the "bored" child is usually not the extremely academically gifted child lacking a challenge. In fact, that is rarely the case. More times than not, the kid who claims to be "bored" is actually frustrated. Either he does not understand the material that is being presented, or he does not yet possess the skill that he is being asked to demonstrate.

Kids (and adults) do not like to admit they are incapable of doing a task they're expected to perform with ease. Neither do they want to acknowledge they haven't the foggiest understanding about something that has already been explained several times. Kids normally find it less painful to claim boredom than to disclose a deficiency. Consequently, the child who says he is bored is often just "passing the buck." He doesn't understand the material. The work isn't fun. And furthermore, he doesn't want to work. He wants to be entertained! In his mind (albeit subconscious), his frustration is the teacher's fault because she isn't making the learning process enjoyable.

The unlucky child learns that the "boredom syndrome" gives his parent a hook on which to hang teacher criticism. The kid tells the parent he is bored. The parent blames the teacher. The teacher reacts defensively. The child continues to flounder. The teacher gets frustrated, and the parent remains angry. And the winner is – NOBODY! When we combine a teacher's defense mechanism with a parent's finger pointing, we have a sure-fire formula for failure.

I suggest if your child says, "School is boring", you should RUN - not walk - to the telephone and request a conference with your youngster's teacher. Advise the teacher of your concern. Assure her you are not requesting a conference for the purpose of assigning blame. Tell her you need her opinion as to what she thinks might be the true cause of your young student's claim of boredom. When approached in a non-threatening manner, most teachers will do everything possible to work with you to determine the cause, and work toward a solution. And furthermore, they will appreciate your concern.

It is easy to say (critics do it frequently) that teachers should provide stimulating, challenging material for *every* child every minute of every day! I personally do not know one single teacher who would not like to do that. Neither do I know one single teacher who is actually capable of achieving such a feat. It simply isn't possible!

I'll use an analogy to illustrate what I'm talking about. We'll pretend a free computer class for adults is going to be offered at the local library. It is advertised as being open to all levels of proficiency.

Grandma Betty received a computer from her "kids" two birthdays ago. The computer is still in the box because the kids live out of state, and Grandma doesn't know where to plug in all those "dern" cords! Grandma Betty quickly enrolls in the computer class.

We'll call student number two, Aunt Barb. For the past three years Aunt Barb has been communicating with her family and friends via e-mail. However, last week she saw an interesting gadget (guaranteed to take off 50 pounds in six weeks) advertised on TV, and the only way she can get it is by ordering through a web site. Aunt Barb doesn't have a clue about getting on the Internet, and she certainly doesn't know where she would put that silly www. address. She decides to jump on the bandwagon and find out what www. means, and how she can go there. Aunt Barb enrolls in the computer class while visions of an hourglass figure dance in her head.

The last member to enroll in the class is Sam. Sam is a teacher at the local high school. He is extremely proficient on the computer, as well he should be. You see, Sam teaches the Introduction to Computers class! Because he is slated to teach the *Advanced Computer* course next semester and hasn't yet learned how to design and create Web Pages, Sam calls the library and registers for the computer class.

Will the computer class instructor be able to meet Grandma Betty's needs at the same time he serves Aunt Barb and Sam? No way. It simply is not possible to serve all of the needs of all students at the same time. The same principle applies to every classroom at every level of learning.

Sometimes however, a child says he is bored, and he really is! He is the youngster who is exceptionally bright and knows (or at least thinks he does) all the material being presented. He picks up new concepts quicker than his peers do. When he reads or hears something one time, he remembers it. But, he is not a creative thinker.

A creative thinker comes up with his own plan for investigating a topic and expanding his learning. He has more ideas to explore and projects to engage in than the regular classroom schedule can provide. There is never enough time for the creative thinker to accomplish all that he wants to.

Most talented and gifted students are creative thinkers, and they seldom run out of constructive ways to utilize their time. The talented and gifted kindergartener might use his "free time" to write and illustrate a story about a recent trip to Disneyland. The academically superior seventh grader might choose to write an essay that compares the Salem witchcraft trials of 1692 with the treatment of American Muslims after the 2001 terrorist attacks. The accelerated high school junior might use his study hall time to search the Internet for available college scholarships, grants and loans. (Most gifted learners can find a "free ride" if they look long and hard enough.)

However, as mentioned previously, not every exceptionally bright kid is a creative thinker. These unique ultra-smart kids who can't, won't, or don't use their giftedness to initiate and plan activities to expand their own learning, ultimately become bored – with a capital "B." Their boredom is real, and it is a problem. Their needs deserve to be addressed every bit as forcefully as the needs of the kids who use the claim of boredom as a cover-up.

You parents who have an exceptionally bright child complaining of boredom also need to solicit the teacher's help. (Remember, Super-Smart kids have problems just like average and struggling kids do. Their troubles just look different and come in different packages.) When you call to make an appointment with the teacher, ask if she thinks it would be beneficial to have your child attend the conference with you. The teacher will take into consideration your child's personality, ability, behavior, and attitude before deciding whether or not he should accompany you to the initial meeting. (It is extremely likely that this type of problem will require more than one teacher-parent visit.)

When you arrive for your appointment (with or without your child), reassure the teacher that you are there to seek suggestions – not to assign blame. Tell her you are looking for ways in which you can work together to maintain (or more likely - rekindle) your child's interest in school. Let her know you need advice on how your child might be encouraged to accept some responsibility for his own enrichment learning. Share with her any of your child's special interests she might not be aware of. Tell her about any methods or situations that have motivated your child in the past, as well as any failed attempts. (There's no sense reinventing the wheel.)

Almost every teacher will go the "extra mile" if he is approached with an, "I need your help" manner. He will be more aware of your gifted child's needs, and he will respond to them with increased effort. Many will use personal time to locate more demanding and challenging learning material for a gifted – but bored - student. They will also search for ideas on how to entice your gifted student into becoming more accountable for his own enriched learning.

When you open the door of communication with a smile, any teacher worthy of his title will walk through that door with your child on one side and you on the other. It makes for a crowded doorway, but the end result is worth the squeeze.

Boredom, after all, is a form of criticism.
- William Phillips

9

THE REST OF THE STORY

A short time ago I had the unpleasant experience of reading an editorial written by Thomas Lucente Jr. of the *Lima* (Ohio) *News*. In his editorial he condemned the results of a national telephone poll conducted to determine the publics' choice of America's five greatest presidents. Mr. Lucente was *very* unhappy with the poll's victors. He stated that "public stupidity" accounted for the results.

Although I regarded his entire piece as ludicrous, I found one particular portion absolutely infuriating. He said, "This poll shows the devastating result of decades of liberal education policies that place self-esteem and political correctness ahead of real learning and critical thinking skills; skills that embrace education fads such as ... and 'whole word reading,' instead of phonics."

I could make some snide remark about Mr. Lucente referring to the "Public" as being stupid, when he wrote a sentence considerably longer than any sentence should be. But I won't. Instead, I want to talk about the part of his "diarrhea of the mouth" statement where he inferred that phonics was no longer being taught in our schools.

This chapter is written in an attempt to give "the rest of the story" about phonics. Hopefully it will clear up some misconceptions that have been giving educators and school systems a "bad rap" for decades.

All of you know that phonics is the association between a letter (or group of letters) and the sound it represents. You understand that phonics is the discipline whereby kids learn that letter "s" represents the sound heard at the beginning of "smart", and the letters "th" represent the sound heard at the beginning of "think." So why do I say that so many people misunderstand phonics?

The misunderstanding is not about what phonics is. The confusion is about whether or not we teach phonics. That doubt is coupled with a fair amount of uncertainty about when (or if) phonics was "reintroduced" into the curriculum.

During the course of my forty-two year teaching career, I heard hundreds of comments regarding phonics. Most were strikingly similar both in content and connotation. A typical one sounded like this. "I'm so glad that you are teaching phonics. My older son is not a very good reader (or speller) because they didn't teach phonics when he was in first grade." That statement (or a slight variation thereof) always puzzled me. And then one fine day a parent said almost exactly those words to me about her sophomore daughter. The problem was, that particular parent apparently momentarily forgot that *I* was her sophomore daughter's first grade teacher. Oh, my!

I began teaching first grade in 1958, and believe you me – I taught phonics. Throughout the course of my career I taught first grade in five different school districts throughout Minnesota and Iowa, and I always taught every single letter-sound association known to man. I left nothing out.

As a matter of fact, phonics was so much a part of my life that it almost caused a divorce in our household when our second son was born. My husband (who likes to claim he is 100% Irish – he isn't) wanted to give our newborn the Gaelic spelling of John, which is SEAN. Well, I stood up for what I believed strongly in. "Sean" was not phonetically correct and such a spelling would certainly have a negative influence on his entire life.

I won't tell you who won the argument, but I will tell you what happened several years later when that "little guy" was introduced as a participant in our state's wrestling tournament. Over the PA system came this introduction: "And wrestling in maroon and white for Independence is, **SEEN MCTAGGART**." (Now you know who "wears the pants" in our family.) But I must confess, it doesn't appear to have affected Sean's life in any negative manner. (I still think *Shawn* would have been better, because that spelling is phonetically correct. Don't you agree?)

But, forgive me. I digressed. You may be wondering what my colleagues were doing while I was attempting to teach that "m" says "mmmmmm" as in the **M & M**'s that **m**elt in your **m**outh instead of your hand. Well, they were doing exactly the same thing I was! I *never* taught with (or even met) a teacher in the primary grades who did not believe that phonics was extremely important in the process of learning how to read. And furthermore, I never taught for a principal who would have allowed any primary teacher not to teach phonics. Phonics instruction was mandatory, and it continues to be so today.

At this point I have no doubt whatsoever that many of you are just plain disgusted with me. You are absolutely positive there have been certain periods of time when phonics was not taught. You may be thinking of a certain school system or an experience with one particular teacher where phonics was not covered. Of course you might be right, but it's certainly not something I ever observed. Now don't give up on me and slam your book shut. I think I can explain how and why this misnomer about eliminating phonics came to be a widely accepted belief.

I believe we teachers are at fault for causing the erroneous misconception that phonics was not or is not being taught in our primary grades. As educators, we have unintentionally caused doubt and misunderstanding through our failure to accurately communicate to the public the way in which we teach phonics. In essence, our heads have been in the sand while we've been muttering and grumbling about the public's perception of phonics instruction having been sent to the crematorium. (Sand on the tongue tastes so yucky!)

Allow me to explain. First we (educators) eliminated phonics from the progress report as a separate subject. Next we started referring to phonics in new, "fancy-schmansy" terms that left the public wondering what language we were speaking in and what we were talking about.

Prior to the late sixties, phonics was taught as a separate subject with a text, a workbook, purple worksheets, and it's own special spot on the report card – or as we call it today - the Progress Report. Every parent knew phonics was being taught because he saw an A, B, C, D, or (heaven forbid) an F marked in the square following the word...PHONICS.

In the period between 1970 and 1975, most schools across the nation waved goodbye to Dick, Jane, Sally, Puff, and Spot and purchased new reading materials. The books in all of the new reading series incorporated a complete phonics program as a major component of reading within *one* text. The text was commonly referred to as the child's "reader." Textbooks previously used to teach phonics as a separate subject were discarded.

When the new readers were introduced, PHONICS lost its lone spot on the report card. Because phonics had come to be considered as one part of the reading process, the marks measuring that skill were included within the READING grade. Unfortunately, a misunderstanding resulted because teachers failed to tell parents they had *not* discontinued the teaching of phonics! They had simply discontinued giving phonics a grade of its own. To date, little has been said or done to clarify these changes with the public. It is no small wonder that some parents believe, erroneously, that phonics is not being taught in our schools.

The effectiveness of today's method for approaching phonics stems from the fact that the child realizes early on there is a reason (besides pleasing the teacher) for him to be learning all of those sound and letter associations. He sees that his new skills allow him to figure out unknown words by himself. He feels like a reader instead of a robot that has memorized a bunch of isolated sounds. He sees himself becoming an independent reader, and he likes the way he feels!

To help us better understand how phonics has been taught throughout this last quarter of a century, I will describe a typical lesson. I'll use the sound of "sh" for our example. When the first "sh" word is introduced in the student's reader, we teach the sound and we "play" with it. We brainstorm all the words we can think of that start with the "sh" sound. (With some classes that is a rather risky endeavor.) We look for words in our library books that start with "sh." We invite kids to share an item from home that begins with the "quiet" sound. The teacher says three words (bell – tell – shell) and the student picks the one that begins with the day's "magic" letters. We rhyme by substitution. (What word starts with "sh" and rhymes with "hop.") When a new word in succeeding stories starts with "sh", we review the sound. Yes, we most definitely teach phonics, but we do it without worksheets and workbooks.

Another reason for the misconception about whether or not phonics is taught, involves terminology. Every occupation has its own terminology commonly used among its members, but totally "Greek" to those of us outside that workforce. I am made keenly aware of this truth when my spread-out family has the opportunity to spend some time together. Son Mark is a masonry contractor and is forever giving us suggestions on masonry projects we might want to do to upgrade the value of our home. I'm not sure if his ideas are any good or not, because I can't follow his lingo. Son Sean (no, not SEEN) is employed with the pharmaceutical industry, and is very helpful in interpreting for us the many medications and possible side effects of his dad's prescription medicines. We certainly rely on his knowledge and expertise, but often have to say, "Stop. Tell us in words we can understand."

Teachers are no different. We too have our own language. When the topic involves phonics, the terminology is mind-boggling. Teachers (or at least the ones I know) hardly *ever* use the word "phonics." Now don't misunderstand. We read, discuss, and ask questions about the various components of phonics. We constantly attempt to find better ways to teach digraphs, diphthongs, phonemes, consonant blends, phonemic analysis, CVC patterns, and on and on. Occasionally, we might include and mark some of these subheadings on our Progress Reports or discuss them at the parent-teacher conference. (And then again, we might not.) So do parents really understand that all this mumble-jumble is just plain old phonics dressed up in new terms? I doubt it. And whose fault is that? (Teachers, we'd better hide our mirrors.)

Reading is like a casserole. It has many ingredients. We must put all of the ingredients into the dish in order to end up with a competent reader. For most children who are learning to read, phonics is the major ingredient. This is the tool that enables them to sound out new words and to read independently. However, kids also need to learn hundreds of sight words that are not phonetically correct. I'm referring to words like *who, what, where, why,* and *Sean.* They must also be taught how to comprehend what they are reading. (Saying words without understanding their meaning is not reading. It is simply word-calling.) And perhaps the biggest challenge of all is getting a child to enjoy reading so that he will choose to read...beyond the classroom door. Because of these reasons, we now teach phonics as a means to an end instead of 'the end.'

I would stop here, but my teacher antenna tells me there is still some grumbling going on out there. I believe I am hearing something like this. "Okay, Mrs. Smarty Pants, if they've always taught phonics, how come my college senior can't even spell 'please send cash' without using the spell-check on his computer?"

Ironically, some very bright children (and adults) never do learn phonetically despite being exposed to strong phonics instruction and excellent teachers. Some kids' brains are simply not "wired" that way. So does this mean they are destined to be poor readers and horrific spellers? Nope! It simply means they will learn to read by sight recognition, and spell by memorization (or use that trusty spell-checker).

Let's conclude with the questions we started with. Do we currently teach phonics? You bet we do. Phonics is taught every single day - in one form or another - to kindergarteners, first, and second graders in almost every school in this country. If you doubt this, ask the principal at the primary level near your attendance center. You may be surprised (and delighted) to learn that what you thought had been discarded, is in fact simply being addressed in a different manner, called by a different name, and included as one segment of the Reading grade.

When was phonics reintroduced into the curriculum? In most schools it wasn't reintroduced, because it was never taken away. We simply taught it differently, referred to it by a different name, and neglected to keep you informed about the changes. We educators are the cause of the misunderstanding, and we accept the blame. We hope you'll forgive us.

I believe once parents understand the way in which we teach reading (and phonics), they will take hold of our hands and say, "How can we help?" (They always do, once they understand where we're coming from and where we're going.) And now you've heard 'The Rest of the Story' on phonics instruction.

Nothing is so obvious that people will not disagree with it.
-Marilyn Vos Savant

10

A WEIGHTY PROBLEM

Frank Deford, senior contributing writer for Sports Illustrated and author of 13 books recently said, "For the long term, the greatest threat to our society is not al-Qaida, North Korea or Iraq. It is the way we choose to live, how much we choose to sit, and how much we choose to eat." I concur with his assessment.

The nationally growing problem of excess weight is affecting today's children in a myriad of negative ways. It's a condition that often causes young people to be labeled as plump, roly-poly, chubby, and numerous other "clever" names. In reality, the kid is *fat*. Of course if we apply "political correctness" (and a moderate amount of sensitivity), we refer to the individual as being overweight or obese.

Before going further, I must 'fess up and admit I personally have always fought the battle of the bulge. Although never grossly overweight, I am prone to tote around more pounds than I would like. About every ten years (no sense rushing things) I decide to do something about it, and I diet to the point where I become too thin. Acquaintances start asking about my health, and insinuate I "look a bit haggard." At my age, one doesn't need any added liabilities. So, I start to eat just a wee bit more. Then, poof! Quicker than you can say "pecan pie with whipped cream," I'm back to where I started. But, I'm not writing this chapter to discuss MY struggle with excess pounds. Nope, this is strictly about kids. (I just wanted to assure you I identify with the problem.)

Although estimates vary, some experts claim as many as 25% of American children and adolescents are overweight or obese. According to Dr. Wendy Wright, director of the childhood obesity clinic at Mount Sinai Hospital in Chicago, this condition has serious health consequences. She states, "These children often suffer from sleep apnea and don't get enough oxygen at night, which affects their school performance, their emotional life and eventually their hearts. Many already have ominously high blood pressures and cholesterol levels."

Obesity also causes or worsens other medical conditions such as type 2 diabetes and joint problems. Overweight kids are being hospitalized for weight related illnesses at a rapidly rising rate. In 2002 the Centers for Disease Control and Prevention reported that hospital costs related to childhood obesity have more than tripled in the past 20 years. The current annual figure is **$127 million**.

In December 2001 Surgeon General David Satcher reported that approximately 300,000 Americans a year die from illnesses that are caused or worsened by obesity. He suggested we might soon see that toll surpass tobacco as the chief cause of preventable deaths. In June 2003 a scientist from the Centers for Disease Control and Prevention warned that one in three U.S. children born in 2000 will become a diabetic unless many more people start eating less and exercising more.

Although not necessarily life threatening, another toll of excess weight is low self-concept. Occasionally we encounter average-size or thin adults who are insensitive to grossly overweight individuals. Kids are often downright cruel to their heftier peers. Perhaps they don't intend to inflict emotional pain, but they do.

More than a few times throughout my teaching career I was forced to comfort a little girl who had just been called "Blubber Butt", or a young lad who was picked last for the soccer game because "he was too fat to be any good." Unfortunately, repeated remarks along these lines leave permanent scars on the ridiculed kid. Being FAT is not fun, and being taunted about it is very, very painful.

Why are our kids getting fatter at such an alarming rate? There are several reasons, one of which is 'automobile feet'. Today, kids don't walk anywhere. It is too hot, too cold, too far, too dangerous, or it takes too much time. So what do they do? They con someone into giving them a ride, of course.

Kids spend too much time in front of the television and computer. They are addicted to electronic toys – plain and simple. They choose to eat "fast food" that's loaded with calories. (I think it's called Fast Food because it puts on the pounds - FAST!) And finally, they show extreme creativeness in their ability to avoid anything remotely resembling physical activity. Dr. Frank Booth, a physiologist at the University of Missouri has a name for this lifestyle: sedentary death syndrome, or SDS.

Granted, there are also some unavoidable conditions that cause a child to be overweight. A substantial number of children are prone to gaining weight because their mothers developed gestational diabetes while pregnant. Gestational diabetes sets up abnormal glucose (blood sugar) regulation and greatly increases a child's risk of being obese. Genes also are a factor. Research shows that having at least one obese parent doubles the likelihood a child under age 10 will be obese. Rate of metabolism also contributes to body fat. Two kids can eat exactly the same amount of the same foods. One is a skinny-minny, and the other is roly-poly. It's one of those

"It ain't fair" parts of life that many of our kids are forced to cope with.

Although we can't change our genes or pre-natal medical conditions, we can change our habits. Because a lot of little things cause most weight problems in children, it stands to reason that some little changes will help to remedy the situation. I would like to share with you (truncated and paraphrased) "Ten Tips for Parents" as presented by Dianne Hales in an article that appeared in nationally distributed newspaper supplements on January 7, 2001.

- **Don't use food as a reward** or a means of shaping behavior. Ask yourself if a child is hungry for something emotional, rather that food.

- **Focus on health rather than weight**. The most successful approach focuses on feeling better, stronger and more energetic.

- **Don't forbid any food**. Let kids keep foods they "can't give up" in a junk-food drawer for an *occasional* treat.

- **Take charge**. Don't turn over food decisions to kids. It's our responsibility as parents, grandparents, and caretakers to provide healthy meals.

- **Watch portion size**. (Ms. Hales suggests one Tablespoon of food on the plate for each year of age.) That sounds like starvation to me! I recommend you use your own good judgment, and discourage (or forbid) "heaping piles."

- **Limit pop (soda) and juice**. Eating fresh fruit is healthier than drinking fruit juice loaded with sugar.

- **Encourage your kids to participate in at least one sport**. Also, provide opportunities for unstructured neighborhood activities such as rollerblading, bike riding, or skateboarding.

- **Set a maximum daily time limit of two hours** for TV, video games, and the computer. (If they whine too loudly, send them to their bedroom with a workout tape.)

- **Avoid weight-loss pills and fad diets**. They don't do much for most adults, and they shouldn't even be tried with kids.

- **Never say DIET**. The word "diet" has the connotation of fixing the problem and then returning to The Good Life. Instead, the goal of a parent should be to help the child make permanent changes by making wiser food choices, decreasing the amount of food, and increasing physical activity.

Because childhood obesity has become a national epidemic, numerous solutions have been recommended as a solution. While addressing the nation about this problem, Surgeon General Satcher called for major steps by "schools, communities, and industry" to fight fat. (I find it intriguing that he neglected to include "parents" in his group of warriors.) This was Satcher's first recommendation.

Jacquie McTaggart

"Schools must provide daily physical education for every grade. Physical education has gradually been disappearing, particularly for older students. Just 6 percent of schools require it for high-school seniors."

I don't want to appear disrespectful (nor do I want to be sued for inflammatory remarks), but I think Mr. Satcher missed the mark – by a mile. Daily physical education for *every* grade is simply not feasible. Devoting more **time** to physical education would necessitate subtracting time from the teaching of academics. Do parents want to sacrifice quality learning for increased physical activity? Schools lack the **space** that would be necessary to accommodate every class with daily physical education. Do taxpayers want to build more gymnasiums? Nearly every school district in the country is struggling with budget problems. Thatcher's plan would necessitate adding hundreds of physical education instructors. Are stakeholders ready to have their money taken away from books, supplies, and equipment so they can pay the salaries of more phys. ed. teachers?

Schools are not designed to be full-time day-care centers, and should not be held responsible for fixing every "ill" facing society. That includes obesity. Most parents realize a more active lifestyle decreases the probability of obesity. Consequently, parents must demand their children engage in more physical activity beyond the school day. That responsibility belongs to parents – not schools. (Are you listening, Surgeon General Satcher?)

Increased physical activity can be achieved by refusing to drive kids places where they can safely walk, and by restricting the time allowed for sitting on their bottoms watching TV or "playing" on the computer. Granted, the parent who has the courage to enforce these changes is going to hear a lot of grumbling from his kid. He may also feel like he is alone on a desert island as he watches neighbors and friends continue their same old "whatever you want, sweetie" habits. But once again – the result is worth the pain.

The other side of the weight control coin is of course healthy food choices – in moderate portions. Once more parents need to act as the "heavy." (It never ends, does it?) School breakfasts and lunches do not contribute to obesity. School offerings are healthy and the portions are small. Teachers (usually) do not bribe kids with cookies, nor do they console them with chips and dip. Can parents make the same claim?

The issue of snack vending machines in our schools is another story. I can see no viable reason for schools tempting kids with candy and other unhealthy "treats" by placing a machine in every (or any) hallway. Vending machines of this nature need to be replaced with ones that offer bottled water and healthful snacks – or eliminate them completely.

In addition to monitoring the proper type of vending machines, schools also have a responsibility to provide information on good nutrition and the selection of healthy food choices. And they must allow some time for teaching and practicing the physical education skills that will increase the probability of a healthier lifestyle.

Yes, schools must get involved in the fight against childhood obesity. But remember this. The master key to solving the problem of childhood obesity is stored in the home. A health-conscious parent with the tenacity to stick to his resolve will see his reward in the form of a thinner, healthier, and happier kid.

Now, I wonder if it will help *me* if I put this chapter under my pillow and read it once in the morning and once at night. Nah, I don't think so. How does that saying go? Oh, now I remember. **"You can't teach an Old Dog new tricks.** " Darn!

I know a kid who thinks a balanced meal is a Big Mac in both hands.

- H. Jackson Brown, Jr.

11

NO ZOMBIES ALLOWED

Two related, and extremely volatile issues have been raging throughout our country for many years. One involves the appropriateness of a teacher recommending that a student be seen by a physician to discuss a focusing problem or hyperactivity. The other concerns the physician's wisdom in prescribing Ritalin - a stimulant designed to minimize the symptoms of these conditions.

Ritalin is sometimes prescribed for children who have been diagnosed as having a condition known as attention deficit disorder (ADD) or attention deficit hyperactive disorder (ADHD). The ADD label is affixed to the student who is physically incapable of paying attention to the material being presented, or completing assigned work. The ADHD label indicates the student has an attention deficit and a hyperactive disorder. He is unable to focus, and feels the need to be in constant motion. He is the wanderer of the classroom, the child who "blurts out", and the one who is apt to pinch, poke, or punch. He is usually a male. He is the youngster who often alienates his classmates and prompts his teacher to consider looking for work elsewhere. He is also the child who wants very much to be "just like the other kids", and stay out of trouble. He is not mean or malicious. He is challenged. And because of his challenge, he is forced to work harder than most in order to succeed academically and socially.

Both advocates and opponents of Ritalin can be found in every segment of society. Parents, educators, physicians, psychiatrists, psychologists, and concerned lay people express widely divergent opinions regarding Ritalin and its related issues. No single group is unified in endorsement or opposition. As individuals, most have strong convictions - both pro and con. There's not a lot of gray area when it comes to AD/HD, and Ritalin.

When first approached with the Ritalin issue, most parents are adamantly opposed. They do not want their child drugged – period. More than a few believe the teacher has suggested medical intervention so that her day will go smoother. In this chapter we will discuss both concerns.

ADD and ADHD are medical conditions unrelated to parenting, motivation, ability, or the desire to learn. The most widely accepted theory suggests they are genetic conditions, present at birth. Contrary to popular opinion, most AD/HD children do not "outgrow" their conditions. However, by eighth grade many have learned compensatory measures that enable them to cope without the aid of medication. Some particularly severe cases require medication throughout the student's academic career. Only a small number of adults take Ritalin.

Teachers often encounter criticism, hostility, or anger when they recommend a parent consult a medical doctor regarding a child's attention-deficit or hyperactivity problem. Unfortunately, it is not uncommon for a teacher to be accused of over-stepping boundaries or "playing doctor" when she broaches the Ritalin topic.

Parents may not realize (or forget in the heat of the moment) that it is a teacher's obligation to inform them about every facet of their child's school experience - including the problem areas. If a child exhibits an inability to focus or hyperactive behavior severe enough to interfere with his learning or that of his peers, it is the teacher's ethical duty to share that information. Avoiding that responsibility might prevent a confrontation, but it would be negligent to do so. Furthermore, it would be a disservice to the child in need of assistance.

In addition to sharing the child's problems, it is the teacher's obligation to explore with the parent every possible avenue that might aid in solving the problem or reducing the symptoms. Recommending a visit to the physician for an exploration of hyperactivity or an inability to focus should *not* be the teacher's first line of attack. However, if all other interventions have been tried and failed, the teacher *is* justified in making such a recommendation.

Although the process varies among school districts, there are many similarities in the way schools seek help for their academic or behaviorally challenged students. Following is a typical format utilized by a majority of schools.

After the teacher has shared her concerns with the parents regarding a child's problems, the process of finding help begins. It normally starts with some behavior modification techniques, and always includes two-way communication between the home and school. If the problem persists, the child's "case" is usually presented to the school intervention team.

A school intervention team (in the business sector it's called a problem-solving task force) normally includes one teacher representing each grade level within the building, the school principal, a child psychologist, and a certified Learning Consultant. Often they are joined by the school's social worker, nurse, speech pathologist, and reading specialist.

The team reviews the child's academic progress through a perusal of test scores and a sampling of his work submitted by the classroom teacher. They listen to the teacher's perception of the student's strengths and weaknesses. Following a discussion and some brainstorming, the team compiles a list of suggestions for the classroom teacher to try. The teacher is requested to report back to the team on a monthly basis with an update detailing the student's progress.

If little or no progress is noted within three or four months, the team often directs the teacher to request a parental signature allowing the child to be tested by a certified school psychologist. If parental permission is obtained, an Educational Specialist then observes the student in the classroom on one or more occasions. Sometime thereafter, the testing procedure begins.

The test involves several batteries (components), and usually takes more than a month to complete. Add another month to compile the reports, and one more month to schedule and conduct a reporting conference. The Intervention Team and parents attend the conference together and simultaneously listen to the Educational Specialist's observations and the psychologist's test results. These reports are followed by responding to any questions the parents might have. Depending on the conclusions drawn, the psychologist may recommend that the parents schedule a consultation with a family doctor or pediatrician. The entire process normally takes several months, and often extends into the following school year.

Because symptoms of AD/HD are almost always evident at a very young age, the typical student referred for testing is in kindergarten, first, or second grade. Parents understand the importance of a child's early years in school, and many are unwilling to wait for an evaluation process that grinds on and on. Consequently, it is not unusual for a parent to ask the teacher, "What do you think I should do?"

Assuming the teacher has fully explained the evaluation process just described, it is not unethical (nor illegal) for her to suggest that the parent might want to forego the testing procedure and schedule an appointment with a trusted physician. She should not insist, and she cannot demand a parent put his child on Ritalin. However, she is fully within her rights to present the possibility as an option.

Occasionally teachers are accused of wanting to "drug" kids for the purpose of reducing classroom discipline problems. Critics claim teachers "want kids on Ritalin so they can handle 20-25 rowdy kids every day." I cannot *prove* that statement to be wrong, but I can tell you in all honesty that such thinking is simply not true.

Teachers do NOT want to face a group of slow-thinking, slow-moving "zombies" every day. They simply want every child to have the best opportunity possible to focus his attention on learning and to refrain from the interruption of the learning of others. That includes AD/HD kids.

I (as well as every teacher I've ever known) can think of few things worse than a school day without the enthusiasm, giggles, laughter, questions, and unexpected occurrences that invariably occur in a classroom. Those are the things that make teaching (and learning) so much fun. And how about the normal acts of mischievousness that crop up every day? Teachers expect those things to happen and they are trained to deal with them in a variety of ways. Children will be children. Talking out of turn, wiggling, and impulsivity are all part of being a child. Such behaviors do not indicate a behavioral disorder that needs to be treated with a stimulant drug, and teachers know it. Ritalin should be considered only when behaviors far exceed the normal limits, or attention span is far less than that of the average student.

I have read absolutely ridiculous percentages in various articles claiming overuse (which equates with abuse) of Ritalin. I will share two of those claims with you, followed by some factual data.

In a September 2001 article by syndicated columnist and family psychologist John Rosemond, a mother wrote, "This is my son's first year in a new, private school. Already his third-grade teacher has suggested that we have him tested for attention deficit disorder. I discovered that **65%** of the kids in the fifth grade at his school have been diagnosed with ADD and are taking medication. This is amazing, is it not?"

A portion of Dr. Rosemond's reply was this, "I am aware of a school in which *more* than **75%** of children have been so diagnosed by fifth grade, so this report is amazing but not incredible."

Despite the fact that I am a devotee of John Rosemond and normally agree with what he says, I have to make an exception this time. I find both the 65% and 75% figures cited not only to be incredible, but preposterous. Until I learn the name of the school and can check the figures out for myself, I will continue to look at those percentages with a large dose of skepticism!

Because the statistics just mentioned were totally out of line with anything I had seen throughout my teaching career, I decided to do some checking. The percentages I will share refer both to Ritalin and similar drugs manufactured under a different brand name. They take into account only the medications dispensed in the school setting through the school nurse. There may be students (known or unknown to school officials) receiving Ritalin in a relatively new time-released dosage that is administered only at home. Children in that category were not included in this data.

The following figures were obtained by using information gathered from one metropolitan school district (K-12 enrollment of 10,862) and four rural districts (with an average K-12 enrollment of 1800 students).

GRADE LEVEL	PERCENTAGE USING RITALIN
Kindergarten through second	3%
Third through fifth	5%
Sixth through eighth	2%
Ninth through twelfth	1%

The above statistics were obtained from schools in the Midwest. Some areas of the country may have a slightly higher percentage of children taking Ritalin. However, I continue to seriously doubt the 65% and 75% figures, or anything even close to that. Chat room contacts with teachers across the country, personal conversations at national conferences, and extensive reading on the subject, lead me to believe the districts I polled are typical of schools throughout the country.

If you are curious about your own school attendance center, I suggest you call your school nurse and ask for the total enrollment figure and the number of students receiving Ritalin or one of its counterparts. Although school officials are not legally obligated to give out such information, I can't imagine why they wouldn't. Schools have no reason to hide (or embellish) information regarding Ritalin. Of course they will never disclose names or relate confidential information about an individual student. Incidentally, if your "sleuthing" reveals any figure higher than 20%, you have the right and the responsibility to investigate the matter further – 'cause something is drastically wrong!

In order to understand the controversy that surrounds Ritalin, we need to take a close look at the drug. I will share the good, the bad, and the ugly. After you have examined both sides, perhaps you will be in a better position to decide where *you* stand on the issue.

Despite a medical diagnosis of AD/HD and a doctor's recommendation to try Ritalin, many parents refuse. Such a refusal is understandable considering the myriad of horror stories attributed to the drug. The list of Ritalin's possible side effects is enough to scare the "bejeezus" out of anybody. In an attempt to learn all I could and present this issue as fairly as possible, I typed in "Ritalin" on my favorite search engine (for me that's Google) and came up with **192,000** hits. While that was a bit more than I wanted to know about the drug, I did check out several sites that were obviously opposed to it. (I already knew the other side of the issue.) I made a list of all possible negative reactions, and the number was staggering. So, find an easy chair, take off your shoes and get comfy. This takes a while.

Reported symptoms the child may exhibit include reduced curiosity, tiredness, withdrawal from social interaction, listlessness, depression, dazed appearance, and inactivity. Reports also indicate a child on Ritalin may appear bland, emotionally flat, depressed, sad, and humorless. And if that isn't enough, add the supposed possibility that a youngster on Ritalin might exhibit a loss of initiative or spontaneity. He could become passive, or develop spasms resulting in tics of the head, neck, face, eyes and mouth. To that you can add appetite loss, insomnia, arrested growth, headaches, delusions, stomachaches, hallucinations, and feelings of paranoia. And the most recent claim (albeit highly controversial and unproven) charges that Ritalin use is responsible for causing children to begin a habit of taking drugs that may lead to later use of "illegal" drugs.

There! I've told you every bad thing (and some are truly horrible) I could find. Taken at face value, that list would cause any thinking person to refuse Ritalin for their child. But, there's more to the story.

Ritalin was introduced in this country in 1956. Two years later, I began my teaching career. Between 1958 and 2001 I taught or was acquainted with scores of children who took Ritalin on a regular basis, and I **never** saw any of the side effects previously mentioned. (I did, however, have some parents report insomnia problems.) Just to make the record clear, I am not suggesting these results cannot occur. However, judging from my experience, I believe the probability of seeing any of these side effects – other than insomnia - is extremely remote!

If you look at the possible side effects of any over-the-counter medicine in your bathroom cabinet, you'll find them to be mighty frightening too! Last summer my mother came to our home for a month's visit. She was experiencing some "irregularity" problems. (Sorry, Mom!) I thought, 'no problem' and headed for the local pharmacy to purchase a bottle of fiber laxative tablets. After I returned home I read the directions:

"Warning. Taking this product without adequate fluid may cause it to swell and block your throat or esophagus and may cause choking. Do not take this product if you have difficulty swallowing. If you experience chest pain, vomiting, or difficulty in swallowing or breathing after taking this product, seek immediate medical attention."

My goodness, I didn't want to watch her strangle. I just wanted something to "keep her regular!" Granted, there is a big difference between a fiber laxative and Ritalin. But my point is this. All medications have **possible** side effects that range from annoying to serious. (If you doubt it, listen closely to TV drug advertisements where manufacturers are required to list all possible side effects.)

If a parent is ever asked to consider Ritalin for a child, I suggest he investigate the statistical occurrence of the harmful side effects before he says, "No." A physician can provide that information, or he can do his own investigating by checking out the 192,000 websites listed under Ritalin! (Come on, smile – I'm being facetious.)

Ritalin is not always effective. In a few cases it has no visible effect, and in rare instances it exacerbates the problem being addressed. However, Ritalin is not the type of drug where one must wait days or weeks to determine its effectiveness. A parent or teacher can usually determine Ritalin's effectiveness (or lack of) within 48 hours of the initial dose. If Ritalin is taken for one week and there are no positive results or behaviors worsen, the doctor almost always recommends the drug be discontinued. When Ritalin fails to produce positive results, a similar drug (often Adderall) is often tried. Sometimes that works, and sometimes it doesn't. If two different stimulant drugs are tried and no significant improvement is seen, the idea of medication is normally abandoned.

In March 2003 Eli Lilly Pharmaceuticals released Strattera, a non-stimulant alternative to Ritalin. Strattera is given in a once-daily dose. According to the American Journal of Psychiatry (Volume 159, Number 11) the drug "significantly reduced core symptoms of ADHD." Symptom reduction reportedly lasted into the evening without causing insomnia. The introduction of Strattera offers another option and possibly new hope for ADHD kids. The trial and error process of finding a drug to help a child diagnosed as ADD or ADHD need not take more than a month. That's not much time to invest when we remember we are seeking a solution to a problem that will affect the child's entire life.

Now let's discuss the "plus" side of Ritalin. Kids for whom Ritalin is effective normally show a marked improvement academically, emotionally, and behaviorally. They are able to focus on their studies and enjoy the satisfaction of being able to keep up with their peers. They almost always enjoy a better relationship with their family, their teachers, their classmates, and society in general. (Perhaps down the road we'll find Strattera offering even more advantages. At this point we can only speculate – and hope.)

Several years ago I had a very special student in my first grade classroom. I'll call her Becky. Becky was a darling little imp with brown hair, freckles dancing all over her face, and a smile the size of Texas. When Becky entered my classroom she was already an old pro at school. She had spent one year in a special needs pre-school room, one year in a pre-kindergarten room, and one year in a traditional kindergarten classroom. Although my first grade classroom was to be

Becky's fourth year in school, she still could not recognize any letters of the alphabet, or identify the numerals beyond 2.

I silently wondered why Becky was being given "one more chance" to succeed in a regular classroom – or more accurately, one more opportunity to experience failure.

By the end of the second day I knew at least part of the reason Becky had failed to learn any academics during her first three years in school. She had NO attention span whatsoever. None. Nada. If I stood beside her and lightly kept a hand on her shoulder while gazing into her eyes, I occasionally got eye contact for a second or two. Something had to be tried – and it had to be fast. Becky was nearly eight years old and just starting first grade. There was no time to lose.

With more than a bit of apprehension, I phoned Becky's mom after school that day, and asked if we could arrange a time for a visit. Perhaps not surprisingly, Becky's mother said she had been expecting my call. She went on to ask if it would it be okay if she came to the school right away. Of course I said that would be fine; inside I was trying valiantly to ward off a panic attack. Parents almost always recoiled when the topic of Ritalin came into the conversation. Suggesting a doctor's visit on the second day of school was not the way to establish a good parent-teacher relationship. But, I had made the call. Now I had to see it through.

Within ten minutes of the phone call, Becky's mother was walking in the classroom door. Tears were streaming down her face as she twisted the straps of her leather handbag. She was even more of an emotional mess than I was! I started to say something that I thought would be comforting when she tearfully interrupted me. "Please, oh please don't tell me you are going to put Becky back into a special ed. room fulltime.

I'll do anything you say," she implored. I quickly assured her my reason for calling was not to find a different room placement for Becky, but to look for something that might help her learn in my room. I explained that I could make no promises, but there was a possibility Ritalin might help Becky focus enough to learn some skills. Would she be willing to talk to her family doctor about the situation? She assured me she would, and walked out the door. It was 3:25 p.m.

The next morning I arrived at school at my usual time of 7:45, and waiting for me in the parking lot were Becky and her mom. Oh, my! Mom climbed out of her mini-van and came rushing toward me clutching a bottle of pills. She breathlessly explained how she had left my classroom the day before and driven directly to the doctor's office. When she arrived she told the receptionist she had an emergency with Becky and absolutely had to see the doctor immediately. Strangely, the receptionist granted her request. (I suspect the tears helped.) She went on to explain how the doctor had advised she not get her hopes too high, but Ritalin was worth a try. (By the smile on her face I knew she did have high hopes. I prayed they weren't too high.)

Fast forward to the end of that school year. Becky was reading text at grade level, although her comprehension was weak. She could write her numbers to 100, count by 2's, 5's, and 10's, add by counting on, and subtract by counting back. She did not master telling time or counting money as well as her classmates did, but she never gave up. Her smile grew from Texas size to the dimensions of Alaska. She saw herself as a learner!

As of this writing, Becky is doing moderately well in a regular eighth grade class. She receives extra help thirty minutes a day from a Resource teacher. She has many friends and is emotionally well adjusted. She continues to take Ritalin. Becky is a sweetheart – a successful sweetheart!

While searching the Internet, I came across a letter from a mother who wrote about her son's experience with Ritalin. There are some obvious similarities between her son and Becky. I would like to share a part of her letter with you. She says,

> "My very bright son's classroom behavior was so extreme he was placed in a special education class for two years. Of course, when we saw that he was in trouble and needed help, we first attended weekly family counseling sessions, and arranged individual therapy for him. Nothing changed for my son. His behavior at school remained the same or worsened. Our home life was tense. When a pediatric neurologist finally diagnosed him with ADD and suggested Ritalin, I was at first adamantly opposed because the idea of such medication for my child went against all I believed in. But nothing improved with traditional methods."

> "I could see my son's frustration at his lack of control, could see his pain at being so marginalized among his peers. I could see his future slipping away. Finally I consented to "try" the drugs, as we hadn't much to lose at that point."

"My son earned his way back into mainstream elementary school after ONE WEEK on Ritalin. If I hadn't seen the transformation with my own eyes, I never would have believed it. After successfully transitioning back into mainstream elementary school, Ritalin enabled him to...go on to successfully complete high school."

- Name withheld

Not every child put on Ritalin has success as dramatic as did the two students you just read about. However, most do enjoy positive results that contribute toward a more successful school experience, and ultimately a better life. If a teacher suggests a parent investigate the feasibility of trying Ritalin, it is because she believes it will help him focus enough to learn, or to control his disrupting behaviors in a manner that will make him more socially acceptable.

Over the course of my teaching career I observed dozens of children make significant academic, behavioral and social gains after being introduced to Ritalin. When that happened, everybody won. The child began to feel worthy and successful. I rejoiced over the "new kid" in my room, and parents resumed breathing!

If a parent and physician agree to try a child on Ritalin, it is imperative the parent maintain close contact with the teacher. The parent needs to know what the teacher is seeing at school, and the teacher needs to be made aware of any changes the parent is observing at home. It's a matter of one partner assisting the other for the benefit of a third party – the CHILD.

I may not have convinced any of you to join me on "my side of the fence" regarding the use of Ritalin, but I feel better for having shared what I believe to be true. I am not criticizing or belittling those who believe differently than I do, and I am not accusing anyone of untruthfulness or a malicious distortion of facts. My opinion is strictly a result of personal observations made while working with a great number of ADD and ADHD kids over a period of forty-two years. My only motive is to make life a little easier for the thousands of children affected by these conditions, and the parents who love them.

When we understand the other fellow's viewpoint, and he understands ours, then we can sit down and work out our differences.

\- Harry S. Truman

12

HOW DO YOU SPELL CNDRGRTN?

Many years ago in the early part of December, a second grader came home from school and said to her mother, "Mom, guess what? We learned how to make babies today." The mother, more than a little surprised, tried to keep her cool. "That's interesting," she said, "How do you make babies?" "It's simple," replied the little girl. "You just change **"y"** to **"i"** and add **es**."

So how do modern-day kindergarteners, first graders, and early-in-the-year second graders "make babies?" Well, they make "b-a-b-e-z," of course. In other words, they use developmental spelling.

The use of developmental spelling (also referred to as experimental, inventive, creative, or transitional) is currently encouraged in most primary grades throughout the country. It involves the practice of allowing the very young child to spell words phonetically, or as they "sound." For example, a first grader might write about his new baby brother this way. "Mi mthr brot hom r noo babe. He kris an ets an pups, bt hez qt."(If you need a translation, ask any primary teacher.)

Parents have a lot of questions about this "new-fangled" spelling. Why do primary teachers allow such an abominable practice, let alone encourage it? How long should this kind of spelling be tolerated? Will the child grow up thinking that any spelling is acceptable as long as the reader can interpret the writer's intent? Do all "experts" agree on this practice? I will attempt to answer these questions in this chapter.

I'll start by telling you that I am in full agreement with the practice of encouraging **young** children to use developmental spelling. I taught first grade for roughly twenty-five years before the practice was begun, and approximately seventeen years after its inception. From my experience, the assets of developmental spelling are far greater than the liabilities.

Teachers who encourage developmental spelling suggest that it...

- Promotes confidence

- Enhances the process of word recognition, which leads to earlier reading

- Enables children to write independently before they are able to spell words correctly

- Encourages writing that is natural and meaningful to the child

You are perhaps wondering if developmental spelling really does achieve all (or any) of these lofty goals. I think that it does.

It promotes confidence as a learner. What did *you* do when your baby took his very first step without holding on to your hand or an object? Did you say, "No, that's not right? Don't hold your arms out like an airplane. Do it over." Of course you didn't! Perhaps you clapped and said, "Good job", and held out your arms to encourage him to try another step or two. And, sensing that his effort was enjoyed (the clapping, the smiles, etc.), he had the confidence to try again.

The same principle holds true with the early spelling efforts of the primary-grade child. If his beginning writing attempts are accepted and responded to without reference to spelling, he gains the confidence to try again. (Hint: If you absolutely cannot decipher the intent of the message, ask your child to please "read" it to you.)

It enhances the process of word recognition that results in earlier reading. Reading and writing are an integration of thinking, listening, speaking, seeing, and spelling. If we isolate the spelling skill and demand perfection at the onset, we inhibit both the reading and the writing process. Kids that are encouraged to spell words using the sounds they hear, are also practicing the sound-letter associations (often referred to as phonics) they need to help them become readers.

It enables children to write independently before they are able to spell words correctly. How many times has your little one said, "Mom, how do you spell (whatever)?" And how many times have you had to respond with, "Not now honey, I'm busy." Transfer that scenario to a classroom of twenty-five kids who have been asked to write a few sentences about their plans for the upcoming weekend. The first child who raises his hand gets the word spelled for him. The remaining twenty-four wait. And how about the second word that student #1 needs help with? Sorry, that must wait until tomorrow! It doesn't take a lot of imagination to visualize lots of waiting and very little writing. (Incidentally, if you employ the "spell it like it sounds" method at home, you'll be doing your child and yourself a favor.)

It encourages writing that is natural and meaningful to the child. Spelling is, of course, a component of writing. Writing is designed to convey an idea, express an opinion, share an emotion, or elicit a response. Can any of these objectives be reached if the young child has not yet learned how to spell correctly? No, it cannot - not if we demand letter-perfect spelling.

No little kid wants to write anything if the content is deemed less important than the spelling. If he is forced to write error free, he will choose words he can spell rather than words that accurately describe his thoughts. The requirement of perfect spelling inhibits creativity, and robs the child of the "private" voice he could be using to share his ideas, dreams, hopes, and fears.

To illustrate, let's look at the papers of two average-achieving first graders who are in different rooms with different teachers. The teachers have diametrically opposing philosophies regarding spelling. Both kids are instructed to write about their favorite Christmas/Hanukah gift. They have thirty minutes to complete the assignment.

The teacher of student number one has a policy that states papers will be handed in when all words are spelled correctly. This is the finished product of student number one. "I GOT A BIKE."

Student number two is encouraged to spell words by using the sounds he hears. This is what student number two writes. "I GT A BOOTAFL NOO BIK. IT IZ RED AND BLAK WTH SLVR STRIPS AWN THU FNDRS. I CN RID IT AZ FST AZ THU WND. I LUV MI BIK."

Both students put an equal amount of time and effort into their work. Which one do you think shows the most enthusiasm? Which tells how the kid feels about his new bike?

Which one do you believe fits the description of "creative writing?" (Remember – we're talking about first graders.)

In the "olden days" a kid wrote on an assigned topic and handed it in. We teachers grabbed our red pens, drew big bold lines through the misspellings, wrote the correct spellings above the errors, and handed the paper back to the student. Of course we didn't comment on the content. There wasn't time for that. Yes, we thought our announce-it-to-the-world corrections were in the child's best interest. But were they? I'm afraid not. The message the child got was, "If you want a good grade, you'd better write what you can spell. Forget about what you want to say."

Today, when little kids are encouraged to spell words the way they sound, they write what they want to share. Their writing is occasionally descriptive. ("Last nit the cat barft on mi bd.") Sometimes it is humorous. ("Dad sed moms metlof tastid lik grownd-up gots met stuk togevr wif gloo.") Occasionally it expresses a fear. ("I wery bowt du tarists cuming two mi town.") Today's primary student writes about what his thoughts and concerns are. He looks forward to the teacher's feedback on the content. And best of all, when he gets his paper back it doesn't look like it's dripping with blood!

Now that you've read all this "fuzzy" stuff about developmental spelling, you may be wondering why you've heard rumblings about this practice from some parents and a few of the "experts." (Or perhaps you're one of them that have been doing the grumbling.) At any rate, there are a couple of reasons responsible for the opinion of those who condemn this practice. Both are understandable.

Number one, this method is different from the way you and I were taught. Number two, many middle and high-school kids are poor spellers and the public needs something (or someone) to blame.

The first reason is easy to explain. Change always requires some adjustment time followed by proof that it works. Because most primary grades have been adhering to this philosophy for about fifteen years, the time element has been satisfied. Teachers see on a daily basis that developmental spelling is successful. Kindergarteners, first, and second graders read sooner and write more. The proof element has been satisfied.

Dissatisfaction with the poor spelling of kids beyond the primary grades is a valid concern, and one that deserves to be addressed. I firmly believe that the practice of using developmental spelling at the primary level does not cause the older child to use sloppy spelling. It does, however, permit careless spelling to continue if teachers don't demand that it be discarded once conventional spelling is taught.

The period of transition from inventive spelling to traditional spelling is generally two to three years. By the end of second grade, students have been taught the correct spelling of most common one-syllable sight words such as *who, what, when,* etc. Of course, the list increases in difficulty each year. The problem occurs when kids "learn" how to spell a word for Friday's test, and then revert back to the phonetic spelling for their everyday journal or recreational writing.

Unfortunately, teachers often let older students get by with developmental spelling because they don't want to thwart their creativity! Perhaps teachers forget (or refuse to acknowledge) that these kids have "developed" beyond this stage and should therefore be held accountable for that letter-perfect spelling we mentioned earlier. I am convinced teachers can, and should, make older kids (third grade and beyond) aware of spelling errors without making their papers look like a road map of red and green squiggles. A light red pencil (pens are so harsh) line under each misspelling that has been previously taught, is not going to cause a kid irreparable harm. In fact, it will do the student a favor! After a fifth grader finds "thay" underlined five different times in one piece of work, he just might spell it "they" the next time. Who knows? He might even be able to spell, "Send money quick" once he gets to college.

Now let's summarize. Developmental spelling is highly beneficial for the kindergartener, first, and second grader. It enhances both the reading and the writing process. Third graders and beyond should be expected to use correct spelling on all final-draft work. And if they don't, their final grade should reflect as much.

If you don't like something, change it. If you can't change it, change your attitude.

-Mayo Angelou

13

POLITICALLY INCORRECT

In the 2000 Presidential election nearly every state and national candidate named education as his primary concern. It started with Republican Geo. Bush who wanted "to leave no child behind." Shortly after the election, Democrat Senator Edward Kennedy picked up the baton in the guise of political harmony, and successfully engineered the passage of an educational testing bill. The newly enacted legislation requires mandated annual testing in reading and math for all third through eighth graders.

The bill was designed to "make teachers more accountable", by providing a scorecard with which to judge and compare the effectiveness of teachers and schools. Senator Tom Harkin (Democrat) said, "The new bill is the beginning of a national effort to reform schools." Senator Chuck Grassley (Republican) called the bill "a victory for students, parents, teachers and educators."

In this chapter we will carefully examine this "innovative" law so that you can decide for yourself whether or not this is an effective piece of legislation. You will have the necessary information to determine if this bill is a victory for "students, parents, teachers and educators", or for the politicians seeking more votes by espousing a commitment to America's goal of providing a better education for all kids.

The law says:

- Students in third through eighth grades will be tested in reading and math annually and the results will be used to judge the performance of their schools.

- Failing schools will receive increased funds, but if scores do not improve after six years, the schools can be re-staffed.

- Students in failing schools could use federal funds to pay for independent tutoring or transportation to another public school – but not to pay tuition for private schools.

The first component mandates the testing of third through eighth grades in reading and math to judge the performance of their schools. What comprises a school? It's certainly more than students alone. In addition to kids, a school functions through the work of the school board, administrators, teachers, support staff, volunteers, and the parents who monitor and support the school's endeavors. Can more testing tell us about the quality or performance of these various components? I find it interesting that the law does not mention the need to learn about student performance so that we might be better able to determine the student's needs.

Long before the No Child Left Behind legislation, schools throughout the country were already spending a monumental amount of time testing kids in order to determine their strengths and weaknesses. They used the results to plan appropriate programs for each child. But now, the government has demanded more. Does MORE mean BETTER?

Most schools currently utilize approximately seven of the required 179 school days in preparation for and administration of various tests and evaluation procedures. This is seven days when the students are not being given any new material or an opportunity to practice an "old" skill because the time is being used to see what students can and can't do. And the government has demanded that we increase the amount of testing time.

My question is, "Why?" Teachers already are cognizant of what kids know and don't know. They need to use their time teaching students new material, and helping them practice skills in the areas that need improvement!

The second component of the law says "failing schools" will receive more money, and if scores do not improve after six years, the schools can be "re-staffed."

Mr. and Ms. Politician, I have a few questions for you. When you label a school as "failing", will you take into account the socio-economic level of the students and their families? Will you consider whether the majority of the students live in a subsidized housing project or in an affluent suburb where the high school kid drives mom's Porsche if his BMW is in the garage being fixed? Will you examine the percentage of students with mental handicaps? Will you make allowances for the immigrant students who have only a minimal understanding of the English language? Where will you transfer kids to when a school "fails?" (Keep in mind that all schools within a twenty mile radius are probably failing too because they are made up of a similar population.) How will transferring the immigrants, the minorities, and the poverty stricken to new schools foster greater learning? Will they automatically learn to understand and speak English fluently? Will their home environments magically become transformed? Will the tooth fairy bring all needy kids a roof over their head, food for their bellies, and a safe haven from drugs and violence? These are the things that affect learning. I'm unsure how your laws will help. Will you explain it to me?

How will independent tutoring or transferring to another school help the failing student (which, when multiplied, comprises a failing school)? Normally, the same circumstances that cause a student to fail in one setting will also accompany him to a tutor, to a different teacher, or for that matter, to a different school. Yes, there are exceptions to that statement. But they are rare.

Saying that "schools can be re-staffed if they fail to improve" sounds an awfully lot like the flexing of the Federal Government's muscle. Do you not realize, or did you just "forget" that less than 3% of a districts' funding comes from Washington? Where does the lion's portion of school funding come from? What happened to local control?

The third factor in this law says that students in failing schools can use **federal** funds to pay for independent tutoring or transportation to another public school. Who supplies the money for these "federal funds?" (We all know the answer to that one!)

I regret having to bring up the unpleasant topic of money, Mr. and Ms. Politician, but taxpayers do have this issue on their minds. The National Association of State Boards of Education estimates that the price of these federally mandated tests will cost states as much as **$7 billion** over the next seven years. It appears you have not yet learned that the participation of the federal government in social programs does not guarantee success. I wonder why past experience has not shown you that we don't solve problems simply by "throwing money at them." Thank you for your attention, Mr. and Ms. Politician. I'll be anxiously awaiting your replies.

Although the amount of money required for this "landmark" law is astronomical, it is not my chief concern. My primary complaint with this legislation is its purpose. It is designed not to help kids, but to provide an instrument for which to "make teachers accountable" by comparing the test scores of their students with the scores of kids from a different teacher, district, or state. (A stipulation has recently been added requiring *every* child to achieve at a proficient level in reading, math, and science by 2014 – a virtual impossibility.)

Of course teachers need to be held accountable, the same as any employee in any occupation or profession does. And whom do I suggest should be responsible for determining teacher accountability? I believe that our school principals should be allowed to accept this responsibility. They have the training, knowledge, skill, experience, and the willingness to do the task. Unfortunately, it appears that these qualities are going to be replaced with tests that will presumably do a "better" job of distinguishing the good teachers from the bad.

Each of you reading this book can probably identify the master teachers in your local school system. You also know which teachers are good, but not great. And you may be able to identify a minuscule number that would be better suited to a different occupation. Did you need a test score to help you form your opinion? I doubt it!

You have all heard the adage "You can't judge a book by its cover." Well, the same thing can be paraphrased into, "You can't judge a teacher (or school) by test scores." One cannot fairly compare teachers in different buildings, districts, or states when the students come from totally diverse backgrounds. Neither can we demand uniform achievement from kids who come to the playing field with vastly different equipment. I'd like you to consider this analogy.

Student group A is from an upscale neighborhood in Cambridge, Massachusetts where the majority of students live in the affluent homes of professional families. Student group B is from Independence, Iowa where the kids represent a cross-section of socio-economic homes and educational backgrounds. Ninety-nine percent of the student population is Caucasian. Student group C live in a disadvantaged area of Brownsville, Texas where English is the second language and the students come primarily from single parent, minority families that qualify for public assistance. Would it surprise you to hear that there is consistently a huge discrepancy in scores among these diverse groups? I doubt it. Furthermore, I don't need to tell you which group ranks at the top, in the middle, and at the bottom. Does this mean the "best" teachers are in Cambridge, the mediocre ones in Independence and the "teachers needing to be replaced" work in Brownsville? I don't think so!

Political proponents of this law (which incidentally passed both houses by a huge margin) are quick to point out that they are not going to compare students' scores, but rather student growth. They indicate that such a method will be a fair way of comparing students from widely divergent socio-economic backgrounds. Let's examine that philosophy and see what we find.

First, we need to look at what "academic growth" is. When a student's test results are scored, he is assigned a number indicating the approximate grade and month at which he is currently achieving. For example, an average fourth grader taking a standardized test in October might receive a score of 42 indicating that he is right on target for working at the fourth grade level, second month. If one year later the same student takes the standardized test – again in October and scores a 52 (fifth grade, second month) he will have made one year's academic growth. In other words, he will have made exactly the amount of academic growth that teachers and parents strive for. If, however, that same student taking the test in fifth grade scores a 46 (fourth grade, sixth month), his academic growth will have been only four months throughout the past year – clearly not what we want to see.

At first glance one might think (apparently politicians do) that measuring academic growth is a fair way to compare students. Proponents say that it doesn't matter where a student is on the achievement scale as long as the comparison is made on how much progress he made in a one-year timeframe. I would agree that such a rationale sounds logical. It is, however, grossly flawed.

Kids do not enter kindergarten with a "blank slate." Or put another way, they do not all enter kindergarten with the same skills, abilities, background, and opportunities. Every kindergarten class includes children with varying levels of achievement, and the gap continues to grow wider (between the high and low achievers) every year they are in school.

Children from extremely diverse backgrounds usually have vast differences in every facet of their lives. Differences in nutrition, experiences, adequate sleep, family life, availability of educational enhancement materials, travel, a safe neighborhood, and yes – differences in innate ability - commonly referred to as intelligence.

These differences directly affect "how much" a child is capable of learning in any given year, (no matter who the teacher is) and for that matter - throughout their k-12 educational career. Normally, the child who has all or most of the advantages and "perks" of a good home and neighborhood will have a head start at learning. He will, in fact, be equipped to "start quicker, run faster, and travel farther" than the youngster who has few or none of what we think of as basic human needs. Kids from deprived homes or neighborhoods will never learn at the same rate, because they are competing with different "equipment" and against stiffer odds.

Yes, there are children from affluent, two-parent, professional families who are utterly abominable students. And yes, there are minority children living with a single parent in the ghettos of New York who are brilliant and earning straight A's. But these kids are the exception, not the norm.

Will a comparison of academic growth really prove to be fairer or more reliable than a comparison of test scores in order to determine a teacher's worth or a school's progress? No, I'm afraid not. It's a different sewer, but the smell is the same.

A discussion of standardized testing used for the purpose of making comparisons and evaluations would be incomplete without reference to the fact that tests can be taught to, thereby making the results invalid. Standardized tests such as the Iowa Test of Basic Skills (grades 2-8) and the Iowa Test of Educational Development (grades 9-11), both of which are currently used in many school systems throughout the country, are redesigned about every fifteen years. Any teacher who has administered the tests one time knows which items or areas cause difficulty for a significant number of students. Some teachers will drill on these problem areas the week prior to testing in order to ensure a better score. Others will stick to the scope and sequence that has been outlined for their particular district and allow the scores to fall where they may. (First-time instruction given one week prior to taking a test does not foster understanding or skill. It does, however, increase the likelihood of a higher score.)

The tests we have been discussing are referred to as being "standardized." Well, they are designed that way but they are not always administered that way. Standardized means that exactly the same guidelines are used by every school and every teacher when administering the test and reporting the results. It is true that teachers and schools are directed to follow the exact guidelines to the letter. I'm afraid that is not always the case, and it is bound to get worse. With the high-stake testing that has been forced upon schools, some teachers and some districts will take the opportunity to "fudge" a bit in an attempt to make their district or their classroom appear "better" than it really is.

Schools are supposed to test all kids of all abilities and include those scores in the reporting. However, according to David Frisbee, associate director of the Iowa Testing Program at the University of Iowa, that is not always done. In a 2002 Associated Press article he was quoted as saying, "Another way of boosting test scores is used by encouraging some students to stay home on test day or not having lower-achieving students take the test."

We also need to take a look at the teacher's guidelines for administering a "standardized" test. They are explicit and definitive as to restrictions and requirements. Timed tests are to be observed to the second. There is to be absolutely no assistance from the teacher. There are to be no provisions made for the learning-disabled child who has not mastered the skill of reading the printed word. In the past, most teachers have abided by these guidelines. Will they continue to? I sincerely doubt it. Once the **Testing, Do Not Disturb** sign goes up and the classroom door closes, it's anybody's guess. Some teachers will make less than honest choices in order to make their students score higher, while others will not. Which would you do if your job, reputation, or salary were dependent on your classrooms' average test score or your students' average amount of gain in student growth?

Yes, schools must be held accountable for producing skilled, competent graduates who are ready to move on to further education or the workplace. However, using a test score (no matter how it reflects on a school) as the sole measure of effectiveness does a disservice to our children, their parents, schools, the community, and the country.

Do politicians really believe they can make valid evaluations about teachers and schools through the use and misuse of tests? Or might they be simply promoting a warm and fuzzy concept that will appeal to voters and earn them another four years in office? Forgive me for being skeptical, but perhaps it's time for politicians to be held accountable.

Secretary of Education Paige in an interview in September 2001 made an astounding statement when he said, "We already know everything we need to know to go in and fix the problems of these kids that need fixing." Well, that sounds like a pretty arrogant statement coming from an ex-college coach/college president/district superintendent who has never worked a day in his life on the front lines of k-12 education. But, if he really does know how to "fix all the problems," I sure wish he'd share that information with his fellow policy makers!

Somehow we need to make politicians understand that there is a world of difference between using a test as a stethoscope to diagnose which children need extra help, and using it as a sledgehammer to determine winners and losers among our schools. We also need to convince them that testing is not teaching. We don't fatten hogs by weighing them, and we don't teach kids by testing them!

No man's life, liberty or property is safe while the Legislature is in session.

- Gideon J. Tucker

14

A SPECIAL WEDDING

A short time ago I had the honor of attending a very special wedding. Of course, all weddings are special. Weddings provide an opportunity to share the joy and the merriment of a milestone. They enable us to witness a happy couple begin their new journey together. And weddings allow us to see old friends and reminisce about past experiences.

But this particular wedding was extra special. Seventeen years earlier, the bride was a student in my first grade classroom. The invitation to witness the most important event of Amy's life was a symbol of the strong bond that had developed during the year we spent together. It was a bond that had been forged despite a bump in the road, and it had endured the test of time.

Teacher-student bonds usually are strong, and they often last a lifetime. I (like most teachers) have attended hundreds of athletic, drama, speech, and musical events to observe the performance of students and former students. Bursting with pride, I usually clap harder and yell louder than most attendees. I've had the honor of attending numerous high school graduation parties, a few National Honor Society induction ceremonies, and several weddings. I have received and responded to dozens of letters from former students who simply wanted to keep in touch. I have also experienced the devastation and pain of attending funerals for three former students. Memories of those students will forever occupy a special spot in my heart.

Several factors account for the strong bonding that normally develops between a teacher and his students. We work, laugh, play, learn, and joke together. Occasionally we cry together. We defend each other, and we comfort one another. We know what makes each other happy. We learn each other's trigger points, and how to avoid them. We share secrets, joys, and sorrows. We are partners by fate. We become friends by choice.

Unfortunately, there are situations when these bonds do *not* form. Occasionally (I think rarely) there is a personality clash between the teacher and the student. The two individuals simply do not click. Each grates on the other's nerves for a variety of reasons. When this situation occurs, not a whole lot can be done about it except to wait for the year to end and hope for a "better fit" the following year.

A much more common cause for a lack of bonding between the teacher and the student is the result of a parent demeaning the teacher in front of his child. The "teacher-is-a-jerk" attitude is occasionally the result of some past negative school experience that the parent has endured. He is convinced all teachers are "creeps" and deserve to be ridiculed. Sometimes a parent's negative opinion of a particular teacher is a matter of joining the crowd. ("Everybody in town knows Old Lady Bigbottom is a loser.") In my experience (both as an observer and as a recipient), teacher bashing happens most often following a confrontational encounter between the teacher and the parent.

It would be the rare teacher indeed (I have never known one) who hasn't at some time, in some way, done or said something that has upset a child or angered a parent. It might have been a "dumb assignment," a "stupid rule," a remark, or a grade deemed to be too low. Whether the teacher is actually wrong, or whether the child and the parent misinterpret the "offense", is not the point.

The real issue is the way in which the parent reacts to his child's complaint about a teacher. If a parent blindly accepts his child's version of a perceived offense and then proceeds to belittle the offending teacher and/or her capabilities, the teacher-student bond will be weakened. If the parental teacher bashing continues throughout the year, the bond will be forever broken.

I do not wish to infer that teachers are infallible. We make mistakes – a lot of them! We often give an assignment or teach a lesson that turns out to be a disaster. The next time we try something different. We occasionally commit an error in judgment. We admit our mistake, and vow not to repeat it. We try new methods. Some work and some don't. Sometimes we are required to make a discipline decision in haste, only to discover later that our choice of action was unwise. And the list goes on.

Parental reaction to teacher failures (real or perceived) firmly and almost irrevocably sets the tone of the teacher-student relationship for the remainder of that school year. Sometimes a student carries his negative attitudes about teachers with him as he moves on through the grades. A kid's "Stupid Teacher" mindset can be compared to a tennis ball rolling down a muddy hill. Every revolution picks up more dirt and when the ball reaches the bottom – it is no longer fit to be used in a match.

When your child comes home from school with a complaint about a teacher, your first obligation is to listen with undivided attention. After he has given his version of the situation, and after you have done a little questioning, you may feel you need to contact the teacher to get his side of the story. And then again, you may not.

If your child's complaint appears to be a simple utterance of disapproval, acknowledge the fact he is unhappy with the teacher – and then let the matter drop. (There's no sense in beating a dead horse.) And besides, maybe the teacher (or your kid) was simply having a bad hair day!

If you believe your child's grievance represents a serious teacher infraction, tell him you will look into the matter further. Assure your youngster he did the right thing by bringing his complaint to your attention. Avoid "taking sides" on a kid-griping-about-teacher issue until you have heard both sides of the story. (You just might end up eating crow, and crow is terribly hard to digest.)

Occasionally a teacher angers a parent for some reason unrelated to anything the child has reported. That was the case when Amy (the bride) was in my classroom. It happened the morning following the issuance of the year's first Progress Report.

In the COMMENTS section of the report I had written, "Amy has developed a habit of making inappropriate facial expressions and disparaging gestures to classmates with whom she is displeased. I would appreciate it if you would discuss this situation with her." (When she was disgusted or unhappy with a classmate she would stick out her tongue, roll her eyes, clasp her forehead, pinch her nose, etc.)

The following morning Amy's mom (who happened to teach in the same building I did) came charging into my room long before the first bell rang. She was VERY angry. She told me that Amy's dad (the librarian in our building) shared her sentiments. They were appalled by the fact I had put my concern about Amy in writing instead of speaking to them about it personally. I was shocked and hurt by mom's reaction. I could barely speak (highly unusual for me). I managed to choke out something about being sorry they felt that way. I explained I had reacted to the incident in a similar fashion to what I would have done with a child whose parents I did *not* see on a daily basis. Mom (understandably) was not placated by my explanation. She turned on her heels and left. I cried.

I was absolutely, totally miserable over the entire incident. And furthermore, I knew I was wrong. I should have spoken to either or both of Amy's parents (or any other offending kid's parent) about my concern before, or instead of, putting it into print. I had been shortsighted and insensitive, and I knew it. I ruminated about the possibility that I had forever lost the valued friendship of two teaching colleagues. But more than that, I worried about the affect our disagreement would have on Amy.

I assumed my insensitive error had prompted a verbal tar and feathering the previous evening, and I imagined it had been conducted in Amy's presence. I also expected it would continue in one form or another for the remainder of the year.

If my assumptions were correct, my up-to-then good relationship with Amy would be lost. She would no longer respect me or value my acceptance of her. She would not exert any extra effort to learn. She would have no incentive to make me proud of her because she wouldn't give two hoots or a holler about my opinion. I would probably never again hear her mimic me with her daily enactment of "Today I'm the teacher." She wouldn't even care if she got one of my coveted bear hugs! The end result would be a long, lack luster, minimal learning year for Amy.

Thankfully, my fears didn't materialize. While I was still drying my eyes and trying to regain my composure, Amy came bouncing into the room displaying her usual bubbly smile. She scurried to the front of the room where I was writing the Daily News on the blackboard and said, "Mom and Dad are so proud of my Report Card. They said my grades show I am working very hard. And by the way, they said something about me making mean faces and stuff to my friends. I'm going to try real hard not to do that anymore." (She really did try hard, and within a few short weeks was "cured.")

I can only imagine what Amy's parents must have said about me in the privacy of their bedroom. Thankfully, they did not share their annoyance with me in front of their child. Amy was totally oblivious about the doubts her parents were experiencing concerning my lack of sensitivity and my common sense. They had disguised their feelings so that Amy would not pick up on the fact they were very displeased with her teacher. In essence, they left the door open for Amy to learn all she possibly could in first grade, and enjoy doing it.

(Incidentally, after a couple of months of "cooling off" time, my relationship with Amy's parents began to improve. Today I consider them to be among my closest friends, and I believe the feeling is mutual.)

In a perfect world, a meeting between a disgruntled parent and an offending teacher would clear up all misunderstandings. All involved parties would part company and live happily ever after. Realistically (as in the anecdote I just shared), that doesn't always happen.

If you remain displeased about a decision or an incident after you have visited with your child's teacher, be prepared to bite your tongue – hard! Tell your child you have discussed the situation with "Mrs. Jones", and although you aren't in total agreement with her, she is doing what she feels best. It is helpful if you can at least force yourself to express respect for the teacher's motives. It is **doubly** helpful when you let your child know you expect him to show that same respect. (It's called, "Like it or not - I don't care. Do it or not - I do care.")

I admit it takes a mighty big person to express support for someone about whom we are less than enthusiastic. However, parents are expected to make sacrifices in the best interests of their children. This is just one more to add to the list. Why? Because teachers love to go to weddings of former students!

Yes, I attended Amy and Dustin's wedding with a smile on my face, tears in my eyes, memories on my mind, and love in my heart. That day Amy's facial expressions reflected only pure joy and utter happiness. And ironically, she was still making gestures with her hands.

As Amy proceeded down the isle holding on to her dad's arm, she stopped momentarily by my seat at the end of the pew. She gently squeezed my shoulder, and gave me the "thumbs up" sign. For me, that simple gesture of love was worth more than all of Michael Jordan's real estate holdings or Bill Gates' stock options. It was a priceless gift I would not have received if her parents had chosen to discredit me in front of their child.

A hundred years from now it will not matter what my bank account was, the sort of house I lived in, or the clothes I wore...but the world may be different because I was important in the life of a child.

-Anonymous

15

THANK YOU, TEACHER

Excuse me. May I please have your full, undivided attention for the next ten minutes? (Make it five if you're a fast reader.) I have a very important question for you. I also want to advise you of a national epidemic sweeping our country, and solicit your help in achieving a cure. Let's start with the question.

Do you ever struggle with ways to keep your kids contented and occupied when they are on their winter break from school? I'll bet the answer is, "YES." How do I know? I know because I've been down that road with my own two boys. Although memory tends to weaken with age, I have no trouble whatsoever recalling those days.

The little kids complain about having nothing to do (pardon me...what about all those toys you got for Christmas or Hanukah?), and the big kids want to hang out with their buddies all night and sleep all day. Read on, because I think I have a solution to your problem.

Suggest (no, I take that back...DEMAND) that your child write a Thank You note to everyone who has given him a gift via the mail or by some means other than direct contact. Yes, I know. Kids hate to write Thank You notes. The typical kid almost always suggests a number of things he absolutely must do before he writes his notes. I strongly suggest you don't buy into that line of malarkey. The kid is attempting to delay the task of note writing with the hope you will eventually quit your harping, and forget about it. He figures he will give his scheme a try and wait to see what happens.

The next time your youngster attempts to sidetrack you away from the Thank You note issue, put your foot down. Tell him what the consequence will be if he chooses not to fulfill his note writing in a timely manner. Make certain your consequence is unpleasant, and be prepared to enforce it. (Threats seldom enforced are useless when it comes to modifying behavior.)

The consequence might be in the form of grounding (for the remainder of the winter break), or it could be denying a particular privilege the child enjoys. A total restriction from the computer, telephone, or car would most definitely encourage compliance. I'm sure you can think of other equally distasteful ideas.

When you issue your ultimatum there are a few things you will want to keep in mind.

- The consequence should be more painful (emotionally) to the child than it is to you.

- Be prepared to make *no* exceptions to the consequence until the Thank You notes are written.

- Lift the "sanction" immediately after the notes have been put in the mail.

- Be primed to repeat the process when another "gift occasion" rolls around, because it normally takes two or three sessions of "behavior modification" before a kid decides you mean business!

As an adult, you realize that using good manners (or failure to use them) helps define who we are. Manners (good and bad) become a part of our character and our value system. And that brings us back to the "national epidemic" I referred to earlier. **The exercise of common, everyday good manners is disappearing from today's society**.

During my lengthy career in the classroom I observed a drastic decline in what we call "Good Manners." I have absolutely no answers as to why this has occurred. I don't even have any theories - unusual for me. The fact remains it has happened, and we need to make an attempt to correct the situation.

A written Thank You is only one small part of good manners. Good manners are the cornerstone of courteous behavior. They provide the impetus to say the words and exhibit the behaviors that distinguish us humans from the rest of the animal kingdom. Good manners show consideration for others. They include (but are not restricted to) words like "Please", "Thank You", and "Pardon Me."

Good manners demand that intentional sounds of physical relief such as belching and "fluffing" are saved for non-public areas. (You male readers may call "fluffing" by another name, but I'm sure you get the idea.) Good manners encompass all the things that make the people around us feel good. They compel us to eliminate words, sounds, and actions that cause others in our presence to feel uncomfortable. In essence, they enable us to be an accepted member of a civilized society.

Reading Specialists often advise teachers to remember one irrefutable truth about reading comprehension. They tell us, "Because comprehension skills are not automatically caught, they must be taught." I believe the same thing holds true in reference to good manners.

A child or adolescent does not magically discover on his own the fact that common decency and politeness help to make him a more socially acceptable person. Neither does he understand that those attributes will ultimately contribute to his success, and help to make him a happier individual. He must be taught those concepts.

Every classroom has two or three children who almost always remember the basics of good manners. "Please", "Thank You", and "Good Morning" roll off their tongues as easily as ice cream goes down a sore throat. Teachers normally spend an entire year trying to instill those same good manners in the rest of the class – the ones who never say "Thank you", the ones who simply grunt in reply to "Good morning, Mary", and the ones who greet their buddies with a forced belch. Teachers use various methods to approach this problem, but their goal is the same. They want the student to develop a more acceptable way of interacting with the people around him.

In my classroom I always told the students that if they neglected to say "Thank you" when given a birthday treat, the giver had the right to reclaim his treat! Of course, that threat never came to fruition. When the treat-giver began to extend his hand for retrieval, the recipient would immediately "remember" her good manners.

Was my method effective? Did most of the kids instinctively remember their good manners in the month of May any better than they did in September? No, not really. And why didn't they?

I do have a theory in regard to this area! Good manners, like most values, must be demonstrated and lived in the home if they are to become a permanent part of the child's character. Seven hours a day for nine months of the year is not an adequate amount of time to really and truly instill any lasting principles. (In one year, the average kid spends 1,253 hours in school and 7,507 hours out of school.) Yes, teachers can force compliance ("we'll take your treat away"), but we can't make it an automatic, knee-jerk response.

What do I suggest? I propose parents practice the same good manners at home as they do in public. Kids simply hear messages that are delivered in a lecture. They internalize that which they observe. Parents must therefore "practice what they preach" if they want the value of good manners to become a part of the child's moral fiber. And they should begin this process when the child is very young. Politeness and good manners open the door to a successful and happy adult life. We need to give our kids the legs that will enable them to walk through that door.

Thank you for listening. **Excuse me** if I repeat myself in an attempt to get my point across. **Forgive me** if I have offended you by insisting that instilling good manners is primarily a parental responsibility. (I'll continue to believe it though, even if you are offended.) **Please** understand that my goal in this chapter (and throughout the entire book) is to enlighten and offer practical suggestions that I believe will be beneficial to your child. **Good luck!**

Life is not so short but that there is always time enough for courtesy.

- Ralph Waldo Emerson

16

GOD BLESS THE U.S.A.

Do you cringe when you hear messages like this? "By 12th grade, U.S. students score well below teenagers in almost every other developed country on math and science tests." (Reader's Digest, September 2001.)

Most Americans experience disgust, disbelief, or anger when told their kids don't "measure up" to students from other countries. We love our nation, and through taxes we spend a great deal of money to support our educational endeavors. We wonder what is wrong. Who's to blame? How can we fix it? To answer these questions, we must first examine our country's attitude about which kids we want to educate, and *what* it is we want them to learn.

Countries vary greatly in their attitudes about childhood, how to conduct education, and who "deserves" an education. Most countries in Europe, and many in Asia, traditionally use stiff national exams to sort out students at the end of elementary or junior-high education. The select few who pass the exams are allowed to enter a specialized high school where the student body is made up of "the best and the brightest." Their high schools are operated solely for the purpose of preparing students for entrance to a university. Consequently, **only the top students from high-scoring countries take the tests used to make international achievement comparisons**.

By contrast, Americans believe that *every* child deserves an education. And because of this belief, *every* student's score in America is used to compile our national average. One doesn't need to be a genius or hold a doctorate degree to understand that the "average" score of ALL students (in America) will consistently be lower than the "average" score of the "best and the brightest" students from other nations.

Unfortunately, there is no shortage of statisticians who compare student test scores from nations around the world, but fail to identify the major differences that exist among the student populations tested. Neither is there a shortage of people who are eager to report this incomplete and misleading information to the public. I suspect neither of these groups is intentionally trying to deceive the American public, but that is the end result. Perhaps "number crunchers" and reporters should look beyond the figures, and focus more on the details. It would increase understanding, prevent misinterpretation, and enable the American public to look at these scores without embarrassment, anger, or an urge to apologize.

In addition to educating all kids, Americans feel that it is important to educate the WHOLE child. We want him to participate in organized sports and engage in after-school activities. We want her to be creative, spontaneous, and caring toward others. We encourage him to challenge unreasonable authority. We allow her to watch a great deal of TV, and spend countless hours on the computer or playing video games. We enable him to spend weekends in leisure pursuits, to have his own car, and to begin dating at an early age.

As individuals, we have differences in opinion on students working. However, as a nation, we apparently believe that it's worthwhile for young people to gain work experience and to learn how to handle their own money. Consequently, our young people are more economically active than their counterparts from other countries (Japan, for example).

Obviously, student hours spent in the workforce are hours NOT spent in studying - and test scores will show it.

As a country, we are firmly committed to the breadth of education. In America, our elementary kids study considerably more than the 3 R's. They are introduced to the Arts, required to engage in physical activities that promote good health, and participate in service projects. Students in America's high schools are offered a wide range of courses. They are required to take the basic ones, and encouraged to sample a variety of the electives.

These are the qualities we believe in, and our schools are operated to promote these qualities. American schools provide a well-rounded education and attempt to avoid the stress of subservient conformity that is demanded by students in many of the high-scoring countries. Yes, American kids do score lower on tests than do the kids from other industrialized nations. American kids also have a considerably lower teen-suicide rate. Would you want to see these roles reversed? Of course you wouldn't!

Do our combined, unique American values affect student test scores? You bet! Do I suggest we change our values, or educate only the "cream of the crop" so we can be more globally competitive? Absolutely not. We simply need to understand *why* our kids test lower, and ignore the temptation to make apologies for it. It is not a problem that needs to be fixed. It is, however, a situation that needs to be understood.

American students have a knowledge base that is broader and deeper than students from other countries, but they do not have as much detailed knowledge of specific academic subjects. Fortunately, most acquire this knowledge over time and through experience. Americans need to understand that the destination is the same for our kids as it is for the kids from higher scoring countries. The difference lies in the fact that our road to that destination is much more crowded because *every* kid is traveling it, and each is carrying a heavy load of life-enriching values. I wouldn't want it any other way. Would you?

Before you accuse me of "sugar-coating", allow me to go one step further. Our American education system is not without problems. We have inequity in our educational opportunities, an unacceptable dropout rate, and a continuing dilemma with violence and drugs. Yes, we most certainly have work to do and improvements to make. However, we must make certain that our efforts target the right areas. Raising test scores to compete with nations whose philosophies differ from ours is not a justifiable pursuit. Instead, we need to work together to look for ways that will make education better for *all* kids, and still not abandon the values that we all hold near and dear. Americans have 53 million reasons to hold their heads high, and they come in all sizes, shapes, and colors. They are today's students.

I hope the examination of this issue will prevent all of you from cringing the next time you read screaming headlines about the abysmal ranking of U.S. students. Yes, our kids do rank lower than students from other countries. Our nation's philosophy does not generate the high levels of subject matter achievement attained in some countries by the select few. It does, however, provide every kid with a broad education and a value system that enables him to become a contributing member of society. We have ample reason to be proud of our schools, and the kids who attend them!

Perhaps Lee Greenwood's award winning patriotic song, *God Bless the USA*, says it best.

"I'm proud to be an American where at least I know I'm free.

And I won't forget the men who died, who gave that right to me.

And I'd gladly stand up next to you and defend her still today.

'Cause there ain't no doubt I love this land, God bless the U.S.A."

Teaching kids to count is fine, but teaching them what counts is best.

- Bob Talbert

17

MOUSE POTATOES

Does this sound familiar? "Max (age 4) absolutely loves playing on his friend's computer. I think we should get one so he can play on it at home." Or, "Kids need technology to compete in the global marketplace. We might as well get started now." (Oldest child is in kindergarten.) How about this one? "Almost everybody in Veronica's class (second grade) has a computer in their home. If we don't get her one or allow her to use ours whenever she chooses, she most certainly will be at a disadvantage."

If any of these statements (or similar ones) have come from your lips, you are in the majority. All parents want their kids to have the advantages that will put them on an equal playing field with their peers. (They really want them at the head of the pack, but we'll pretend we aren't aware of that.) Many parents are willing and eager to sacrifice their own pleasures in order to provide that which they think will insure their child's academic success. Is that admirable? You bet! Is it realistic? Read on.

Today's parents are aware of the importance of computers and the integral part they play in our modern day society. Unfortunately, this awareness is prompting some faulty thinking about when we should introduce the child to the computer and the amount of time we should allow him to spend there. Booming software sales of academic programs for preschoolers indicate parents (and grandparents) think the sooner a kid gets his hand on the mouse, the better. And because he is utterly enthralled by all the bells and whistles, we allow him to set up permanent residence in front of the monitor. "So," you might ask. "What's the problem?" The problem is, we are rearing a generation of 'MOUSE POTATOES'.

Many parents believe introducing a child to the computer at an early age gives him a "leg up" on the competition. Some feel that buying mega bundles of software designed for "little tots" is a worthwhile investment because it strengthens the likelihood of success. A large number of 'modern' parents allow their child to spend unlimited hours at the computer because "he loves it so much." (It also keeps him occupied. It's like having a babysitter that doesn't raid the 'frig.)

In the mid-eighties a few schools began installing computers at the high school level. Soon thereafter, highly educated and affluent families purchased personal computers for home use. The following decade resembled a marathon. Schools tried to see who could buy the largest number of computers and the most software in the least amount of time. (Teacher training was not a part of the maiden race, but is currently being addressed.) Parents put off vacations and cut back on their discretionary spending in an effort to keep Johnny on the same technological field as the Jones' kid.

Today, nearly every classroom in the country houses one or more computers, and most schools have computer labs. Currently, fifty-six percent of school age kids in America come from homes with one or more computers. Pop culture might say, "We've come a long way, baby!" Regrettably, the road we have traveled contains some potholes.

In the November/December 2001 issue of *Scholastic Parent & Child* magazine, there appeared an advertisement for "Software & Tech Toys." It included an outline for computer use, age by age. This is what was written about the 18 months to 3 years age group.

"At about 18 months, children first begin noticing that they can have an effect on objects on the screen by moving the mouse. Some software programs can let a child press any key on the keyboard to hear a favorite song or discover pictures and animations. Age two and a half is a real turning point when it comes to using computers and smart toys: Not only can children this age sit for a bit longer, but they are developing the fine-motor control to use things like a mouse."

I can sum up my attitude about this advertisement and their timeline in one word - GARBAGE! Between eighteen months and three years, a toddler develops his ability to discriminate by banging on pots and pans and rearranging the spice rack. When he stacks blocks up and knocks them down, he is developing his eye-hand coordination. When he makes a mess with play-dough and finger paint, he is sharpening his dexterity skills. If he is encouraged to make mom a necklace out of colored pasta and a glow-in-the-dark shoelace, he learns to be persistent. When he becomes engaged in a "share the chair" book experience with a caring adult, his attention span increases. And if he is very lucky, he practices some social interaction skills by virtue of having a sibling or daycare pal play along beside him. (Toddlers don't play together. They simply occupy the same space.)

The very young child needs to learn to coordinate both sides of his body and brain. Using one hand to work a mouse does not satisfy that requirement. It is extremely limiting, and is not appropriate for early skill development. **I can think of no valid reason to put an eighteen-month to three-year old child on a computer – ever!**

I do not mean to infer that after three years of age you can safely and with good conscience plop your little one in front of the computer screen and in essence say, "Go for it!" In fact, my position is quite the contrary. Parents and teachers have a responsibility to kids of all ages to distinguish what's beneficial to children, from that which simply makes them happy. Although computers are fun and engaging, they are not always the most appropriate learning tool. Allow me to explain why I believe this to be true.

The computer allows a child to isolate one's self from family and friends. Computer games are enticing, colorful, entertaining, and non-judgmental. Consequently, kids often find these games more desirable than spending time under parental scrutiny or sibling rivalry. Some kids find the company of a computer preferable to that of a playmate because there are no disagreements to work through. Which option do you think is going to better prepare kids for the social nuances that are an integral part of life? (Some would call that question, 'rhetorical'. I prefer to call it a 'no-brainer'.)

The computer stifles learning and creativity. The instant gratification provided in almost all computer software for kids (bells ring, whistles blow, etc.) when the answer is "right", stifles learning and creativity. If the bell doesn't ring or the whistle doesn't blow, kids simply click the mouse on a different response. After the click, they wait to see if they *guessed* the answer that will give them the desired feedback. With a click of the mouse they have lost the opportunity to observe, think, ponder, and reflect.

The computer provides little or no opportunity for the child's verbal skills. The kid sits in front of the computer screen. He looks. He clicks. He listens. And the process is repeated, again and again. At no point is he permitted to ask a question, to offer an opinion, or to share an idea. He does not talk. He doesn't even whisper!

At the risk of appearing simplistic, I will remind you that talking *always* precedes reading. Communicating with a real live person is a prerequisite to reading. That is how kids first learn to differentiate sounds. (The lion says 'grrrrr' and the cow says 'mooo'.) That is also the way they learn to interpret feelings. ("Johnny, **stop** that this instant!").

Listening to, and repeating nursery rhymes is the way in which kids tune their ears to the very important pre-reading skill of rhyming. Kids begin to develop their comprehension skills through listening to and responding to the spoken words of a real, live person. It is far more effective than hearing the same phrase repeated again and again and again from the 'puter.

We all know that kids have to walk before they can run. We need to remember that they also need to converse (a lot), before they can read. We should not fool ourselves into believing fancy software pre-reading programs can equal the benefit of quality conversation between a child and a caring adult. There is no comparison. The software loses.

Computers provide no physical activity. Although no one questions this statement, many fail to consider its importance. Lack of physical activity comes with a huge price tag. Kids gain weight (occasionally to the point of obesity), and they fail to develop good muscle tone. They miss the fun of learning and participating in a sport or outdoor activity. They miss the opportunity to create and develop friendships that are a byproduct of active play. Ultimately, they end up in the "loser's" bracket of childhood.

Computers are addictive. I have firsthand knowledge about computer addiction, and I'll venture a guess that many of you do too. On many occasions my husband has ambled back to the computer room around 6:30 in the evening and asked, "What's for dinner?" Oops, I have to confess that I got carried away with some intriguing stuff on the Internet, and time just slipped away. Then in a lame effort to avoid kicking myself in the backside, I reason that I'm a big kid and I've earned the right to one or two harmless addictions.

But kids aren't big and they haven't "earned the right." Furthermore, a kid's addiction to the computer is not really harmless. When a kid spends endless hours at the computer he avoids (subconsciously) some valuable experiences. He inevitably misses some (or several) of the activities that will enable him to become a happy, healthy, productive, and socially acceptable adult. He is a spectator of life instead of a participant.

Computers are redefining how we interact with others and how we gain knowledge about the world. Most changes that have come about since the advent of the computer are for the good, but that is not true of all changes. Perhaps it is time for us to embrace the benefits, and discard the liabilities.

We should use the computer as a supplement for our child's formative years, and not allow it to become a cure-all electronic babysitter. When we accept responsibility for our kids' computer use, we can reduce potential hazards by allowing our kids access to some old, but positive learning experiences. We must not fool ourselves into thinking we can replace valuable childhood activities with computer games. There is no software on the market that can offer the same advantages as a picnic in the park, a library card, a visit to the zoo, or a family-shared board game.

An enormous amount of studies have been conducted on the effect of computers on kids. For those of you who would like to learn more about this topic, I am including some of my favorite resources. (I like them because they endorse *my* opinion.) One book is, *Failure to Connect: How Computers Affect Our Children's Minds for Better and Worse* by Jane Healy. Another informative book written by Dianne Levin is *Remote Controlled Childhood: Combating the Hazards of Media Culture*. Both are excellent. They can be secured through your public library or on the Internet. An excellent website dealing with this topic is www.allianceforchildhood.net. At this site you will find, *Fool's Gold: A Critical Look at Computers in Childhood.* See? I'm not anti-computer at all! (I just hate to see kids start on them too young, or turn them into "best friend" status at the expense of other worthwhile activities.)

It is infinitely more useful for a child to hear a story told by a person than by computer. Because the greatest part of the learning experience lies not in the particular words of the story but in the involvement with the individual reading it.
- Frank Smith

18

JUST FOR FUN

I think it's time for a little levity and a few chuckles. Be advised that most of this chapter does not come from my brain cells. I cannot take full credit for any of these stories, nor can I acknowledge the persons who should be given the credit. The "gems" that constitute this chapter are personal favorites that have come to my attention over a period of time by means of e-mail. The writers' names were not attached to any of these pieces, and I have been unsuccessful in determining authorship. I hope you enjoy the fruits of their labors as much as I do.

GOD WAS TICKED

Whenever our children are out of control, we can take comfort from the thought that even God's omnipotence did not extend to His own children. After creating heaven and earth, God created Adam and Eve. And the first thing he said was:

"Don't."

"Don't what?" Adam replied.

"Don't eat the forbidden fruit." God said.

"Forbidden fruit? We have forbidden fruit? Hey, Eve ... we have forbidden fruit!"

"No way!"

"Yes, way!"

"Do NOT eat the fruit!" said God.

"Why?"

"Because I am your Father and I said so!" God replied, (wondering why he hadn't stopped creation after making the elephants).

A few minutes later, God saw His children having an apple break and He was ticked! "Didn't I tell you not to eat the fruit?" God, as our first parent, asked.

"Yup," Adam replied.

"Then why did you?" said the Father.

"I don't know," said Eve.

"She started it!" Adam said,

"Did not", replied Eve.

"Did too", yelled Adam.

"DID NOT", retorted Eve.

Having had it with the two of them, God's punishment was that Adam and Eve should have children of their own. Thus, the pattern was set and it has never changed! But there is reassurance in this story. If you have persistently and lovingly tried to give your children wisdom and they haven't taken it, don't be hard on yourself. If God had trouble raising children, what makes you think it would be a piece of cake for you?

ADVICE FOR THE DAY

If you have a lot of tension and you get a headache, do what it says on the aspirin bottle. "Take two Aspirin" and "Keep away from children."

CHILDREN:

- You spend the first 2 years of their life teaching them to walk and talk. Then you spend the next 16 telling them to sit down and be quiet.

- Grandchildren are God's reward for not killing your children.

- Mothers of teens know why some animals eat their young.

- Children seldom misquote you. In fact, they usually repeat word for word what you shouldn't have said.

- The main purpose of holding children's parties is to remind yourself that there are children more awful than your own.

- We childproofed our home 3 years ago, and they're still getting in!

- Be nice to your kids. They'll choose your nursing home.

Birds and Bees

A father asks his 10-year-old son if he knows about the birds and the bees.

"I don't want to know!" the child says, bursting into tears. "Promise me you won't tell me!"

Confused, the father asks what's wrong.

"Oh, dad," the boy sobs. "When I was six, I got the 'There's no Santa' speech. At seven, I got the 'There's no Easter Bunny' speech. When I was eight, you hit me with the 'There's no tooth fairy' speech. If you're going to tell me that grownups don't really have sex, I'll have nothing left to live for."

TIGHT BOOTS

A teacher was helping one of her kindergarten students put his boots on. The little boy asked for help and Teacher could see why. With her pulling and him pushing, the boots still didn't want to go on. When the second boot was on, she had worked up a sweat. She almost whimpered when the little boy said, "Teacher, they're on the wrong feet." She looked, and sure enough, they were. It wasn't any easier pulling the boots off than it was putting them on. She managed to keep her cool as together they worked to get the boots back on - this time on the right feet. He then announced, "These aren't my boots." She bit her tongue rather than get right in his face and scream, "Why didn't you say so?"

Once again she struggled to help him pull the ill-fitting boots off. He then said, "They're my brother's boots. My mom made me wear 'em." Teacher didn't know if she should laugh, cry, or yell! Finally she mustered up the grace to wrestle the boots on his feet again. She said, "Now, where are your mittens?" He said, "I stuffed them in the toes of my boots."

GRANDMA'S GONE

After a Christmas break, a teacher asked her young pupils how they spent their holidays. One little lad wrote the following:

"We always used to spend Christmas with Grandpa and Grandma. They used to live here in a big brick home, but Grandpa got retarded and they moved to Florida. Now they live in a place with a lot of other retarded people. They all live in little tin boxes. They ride three wheeled tricycles and they all wear nametags because they don't know who they are. They go to a big building called a wrecked hall, but if it was wrecked, they got it fixed because it's all right now."

"They play games and do exercises there, but they don't do them very good. There is a swimming pool there. They go into it and just stand there with their hats on. I guess they don't know how to swim."

"As you go into their park there is a dollhouse with a little man sitting in it. He watches all day so they can't get out without him seeing them. When they sneak out, they go to the beach and pick up shells. They play a game with big checkers and push them back and forth on the floor with big sticks."

"My Grandma used to bake cookies and stuff but I guess she forgot how. Nobody cooks; they just eat out. They eat the same thing every night - 'early birds'. They use coupons for everything, food, groceries and trips. Some of the people don't know how to cook at all, so my Grandma and Grandpa bring food into the wrecked hall and they call it potluck. Some of them don't hear very well. They could hear better if they took the buttons out of their ears."

"My Grandma says Grandpa worked all his life and earned his retardment. I wish they would move back up here. But I guess the little man in the dollhouse won't let them out."

The last selection is a bit more serious. I have made a few changes from the original piece. My additions (and deletions) were prompted by my experience of rearing two boys and teaching 1500 students.

A COSTLY VENTURE

The government recently calculated the cost of raising a child from birth to 18 and came up with $160,140.00 for a middle-income family. Talk about sticker shock! For those of us with kids, that figure leads to wild fantasies about all the money we could have banked were it not for our beloved offspring. For others, that number might confirm a decision to remain childless.

Now let's look at what we get for our $160,140. Naming rights. First, middle and last! Glimpses of God every day. Giggles under the covers every night. More love than our hearts can hold. Butterfly kisses and Velcro hugs. Endless wonder over rocks, ants, clouds and warm cookies. A hand to hold, usually covered with jam. A partner for blowing bubbles, flying kites, building sandcastles and skipping down the sidewalk in the pouring rain. Someone with whom to laugh ourselves silly no matter what the boss said or how our stocks performed that day.

For $160,140 we never have to grow up. We get to finger-paint, carve pumpkins, play hide-and-seek, catch lightning bugs, and never stop believing in Santa Claus. We have an excuse to keep reading the Adventures of Piglet and Pooh, watching Saturday morning cartoons, going to Disney movies, and supervising the breaking of the turkey's wishbone. We become heroes just by retrieving a Frisbee from the garage roof, taking the training wheels off the bike, removing a splinter, filling the wading pool, or bringing birthday treats to the classroom.

We get a front row seat to history as we witness the first step, first word, first bra, first date, and first time behind the wheel. We become immortal as we add another branch to our family tree. And if we're lucky, our obituary is lengthened with a long list of grandchildren. We get an education in psychology, nursing, criminal justice, communications and human sexuality that no college can match.

In the eyes of a child, we rank right up there with God. We have the power to fix an "ouchie", scare away monsters, patch a broken heart, ground them forever, and love them without limits. We use this power so that some day they will follow our example, and love without counting the cost.

And if we are very, very lucky, we get to do it all over again as a grandparent!

Good humor is the health of the soul, sadness is its poison.

\- Lord Chesterfield

19

HELP WANTED

Due to swelling student enrollments, class size reductions, low salaries, unusually high turnover rates among teachers, and a graying teacher workforce, our country is experiencing a dramatic teacher shortage. An estimate by the National Education Association predicts that half the teachers who will be in public school classrooms 10 years from now have not yet been hired. The most critical shortages are in the high-poverty urban and rural districts. The fields experiencing the highest teaching shortages are in bilingual and special education, mathematics, science (particularly the physical sciences), computer science, English-as-a-Second-Language, and foreign languages.

A major effort to solve this problem is the introduction of alternative or emergency licensing for teachers. At this writing (Sept., 2003), 46 states, plus the District of Columbia have some type of alternative licensing program in place. Some training programs are as short as two weeks, providing would-be teachers with scant information on classroom management or how to assess a student's knowledge of a subject. Other programs are more in depth. Some require a student-teaching experience, while others do not.

These programs, which have been passed as state laws, are intended to ease teacher shortages by allowing those with a minimum of a bachelor degree and other "appropriate experiences" to teach without traditional teacher training. They are designed to entice people who are in the middle or latter part of some other profession to leave the big bucks and "put on a teacher's hat." They are also intended to encourage increased interest in the teaching profession by minorities and people of color.

Critics of these programs say they allow unprepared, under-qualified teachers to enter the classroom. Proponents respond with the argument that suggests they aren't talking about the guy standing behind the fast food lunch counter, but rather about doctors, accountants and engineers.

Because these laws have been passed or are being studied by individual states rather than at the federal level, there are many variations. On June 12, 2002 Iowa became the forty-sixth state to enact into law a bill permitting Alternative Licensing for Teachers. I will share the details of Iowa's law, because as of this writing it was the last state to pass an alternative licensing bill, and because it is strikingly similar to the laws previously adopted by most other states.

Iowa's plan says that the applicant must:

- **Hold a bachelor's degree or higher**

- **Have worked a minimum of three years in the field in which the degree was obtained**

- **Successfully complete introductory teacher intern courses to be developed by the State Board of Education**

The school district must:

- **Offer employment to the intern licensee applicant.**

- **Provide a mentor, supervision, and support for the teacher intern.**

- **Not overload interns with extracurricular duties.**

Although there are some positives with this plan (particularly the stipulations regarding the applicant's requirements), there are also some serious negatives and omissions. Iowa's plan, like many other states where the legislation has been enacted, does not require any type of student teaching. This means that the alternative licensee might enter the classroom with a vast knowledge of his subject matter, but no experience in diagnosing, planning, or disciplining.

Iowa's plan stipulates that a school district must "offer employment to the intern licensee applicant." It sounds like Iowa is saying, "Did I hear you say you got tired of or was terminated from your job? Don't worry. Hop on board and you can teach our kids." I wonder what will happen when a top-notch applicant that has just completed the rigors of a traditional college teacher-training curriculum applies for the same job as a poor or mediocre alternative teaching licensee. Is this yet another form of "affirmative action"?

Iowa has not yet determined who will provide the "additional needed support" for the alternative licensee, but I will wager a guess that experienced teachers within the system will be the ones to get the privilege. And won't that be pleasant? Veteran teachers who have gone through the rigors of education courses, classroom management, child psychology, curriculum objectives, implementation of technology, and the prevention of school violence (to name just a few areas) will be appointed to mentor and guide the professional guru who has suddenly heard the calling to teach! Ooh, I shiver just thinking about it!

The final stipulation for the district says they "must not overload interns with extra-curricular duties." Now in the Land of Make Believe, that would be super. It sounds all warm and fuzzy to guarantee that the new kid on the block will have a year or so to get acclimated before being stuck with extra-curricular duties. But, school is real. Personnel are limited, money is tight, and all teachers need to accept their fair share of extra-curricular responsibilities. Furthermore, we don't have to stretch our imaginations too far to determine what kind of camaraderie will develop between the existing teaching staff and the alternative licensee if the latter is given preferential treatment not afforded to other beginning teachers.

You may be wondering exactly why teachers are against a law of this nature. Are they afraid of losing their jobs? I don't think so. Remember, there's already a teacher shortage! Are they afraid of being "shown-up" by an expert in the field? Although that is a possibility, it's doubtful. I believe the real reason most teachers object to alternative licensing is because they believe it is not in the best interests of kids – period.

There *are* many people working in areas outside the field of education who have meaningful life experiences and a wealth of knowledge that could be of benefit to students. However, these assets do not erase the fact that an untrained teacher is unprepared to move into a classroom and carry out all of the responsibilities that an educator is expected to assume. Teaching is much more than spewing out facts and figures. Real teaching connects the subject matter to real life situations. It enables the student to see the relevance of the material being covered and to utilize that information for the purpose of understanding the world and perhaps improving it. Teaching is an acquired skill that involves considerably more than extensive knowledge of a subject.

I am reminded of a story concerning a private school in Victoria, Australia. It seems that a number of 12-year-old girls were beginning to use lipstick and would put it on in the bathroom. That was fine, but after they put on their lipstick they would press their lips to the mirror leaving dozens of little lip prints. Every night, the custodian would remove them and the next day, the girls would put them back. Finally, the principal decided that something had to be done. She called all the girls to the bathroom and met them there with the custodian. She explained that all these lip prints were causing a major problem for the custodian who had to clean the mirrors every night. To demonstrate how difficult it had been to clean the mirrors, she asked the maintenance man to show the girls how much effort was required. He took out a long-handled squeegee, dipped it in the toilet, and cleaned the mirror with it. Since then, there have been no lip prints on the mirror. That principal did some REAL teaching!

At this point I'd like you to join me in a reality check. How many nuclear physicists, doctors, accountants, or engineers do you think will choose to leave their profession in order to become a teacher? Will they be ready to live on a beginning teacher's salary of approximately $28,000 (in a high-paying state) a year? Will they adjust to the life of a twelve-hour workday, six days a week? (We'll pretend they take Sundays off.)

If the alternative teacher is entering the profession as a diversion from retirement, how long will he remain committed to this new life? Will he continue to enthusiastically accept the responsibilities of planning, preparing for, instructing and

disciplining thirty or more kids? (A teacher without
enthusiasm is doomed to failure.)

Perhaps if we take a look at the average teacher's life, we
can answer these questions for ourselves. The typical teacher
has a class of 26 students. His class consists of five learning-
disabled students, three with an attention deficit disorder, one
gifted child, two with severe behavior problems, one who
speaks limited English, one on part-time inclusion from the
special education room, and thirteen kids considered to be
"average."

He must complete lesson plans at least three days in
advance and be prepared to modify, organize, or create
materials (with funding from his own pocket) accordingly. He
is required to teach the students, handle misconduct, utilize
technology, document attendance, write referrals, correct
homework (on his off-duty time), make bulletin boards,
compute grades, complete progress reports, document
benchmarks, communicate with parents, and prepare for
parent-teacher conferences. He also needs to supervise recess,
monitor hallways, and engage in mandatory drills for fire,
tornadoes, and bomb threats. And of course he is expected to
attend extra-curricular events that showcase his students.

He must attend workshops, faculty meetings, association
meetings, curriculum development meetings, planning-for-
change advisory groups, and conferences relating to his
particular field. He must maintain discipline and provide an
educationally stimulating environment at all times. If he is
sick and there is no substitute available, he must "tough it
out." He is expected to dress in a manner that will allow him
to fulfill the occasional necessity of getting down on the floor
with the kids to do some hands-on instructing, and still present
a "professional" appearance for the school board member who
might choose to visit (unannounced) that day.

If he doesn't have a doorway that opens to a colleague's classroom, he'd better have an exceptionally large bladder. (It's illegal to leave a class without adult supervision.) Eating too fast had better not give him indigestion because he has all of twenty minutes to use the restroom, wash his hands, return a parent's urgent telephone call, and eat his lunch. He must continue to take post-graduate courses (on his own time and with his own money) in order to keep his certification in force.

He must not yell, scream, or vocalize naughty words when people tell him not to whine because he "has three months off" every year. Sure, he knows school doesn't dismiss until early June, there are a few days of "wrap-up" required, and some workshops to attend. He realizes he must take another college course during the summer so that he keeps current with new methods. And he certainly doesn't forget that he needs to be back in his classroom the first of August to prepare the room and materials for the first month of a new school year. But, it isn't nice to yell, scream, or say naughty words! So what do you think? Will we have a flood of gray-haired "wanabe" teachers knocking at our school doors?

A longtime friend of mine, Jerry Chapman, spent the major part of his working years as a successful owner and editor of a small town Minnesota newspaper. His wife, Dorothy, was an elementary teacher. After their children left the nest they decided to escape the harsh Midwest winters, move to Scottsdale, AZ, and embark on some new career challenges. For the following fifteen years Jerry worked in the school district's printing department and Dorothy owned and operated a Boutique. When they publicly announced they were going to retire, the schools asked them to help out by adding their names to a very short list of substitute teachers. Dorothy agreed rather quickly, but Jerry balked. He had a degree in journalism, but all he really knew about teaching was what he had heard from his wife during the course of their long marriage. However, after a bit of gentle persuasion (and due to his sense of service) Jerry agreed to give it a try. Following his first day in the classroom I was one of the privileged recipients to receive this e-mail message:

August 22, 2001

Yavapai Elementary School

EVERYTHING WAS FINE UNTIL THE KIDS CAME IN!

"If I could describe my first day of substitute teaching in one word, that word would have to be **disaster.** Before taking a fourth grade assignment of my own, I went along with Dorothy for three days just to see how the professionals do it. It was easy; the kids loved me. When I left they all wondered where my wife's "boyfriend" went. Then the phone rang and I was assigned a class of my own...for a whole day. That day, by the way, goes from 7:15 a.m. to 2:30 p.m. and maybe longer if the regular teacher wants you to grade the kids' work."

"When this little Mexican lass showed up early and started being so helpful, I thought, well this is nice. Cynthia told me everything about the class, who did what, who went where, etc. She followed me around the room, right on my heels, and interrupted everything

I tried to do. I thought, 'Well, this will end when class starts.' Little did I know."

"By the end of the day I wanted to hang Cynthia up by her thumbs. She wouldn't stay in her seat. She pestered the boy across from her. She paid no attention to instructions, and then raised her hand when she didn't know what to do. I can't tell you how many times I told her to sit down and shut up. Well, maybe not in those exact words."

"The teacher left a very detailed lesson plan. Another sub came in just before school and showed us his lesson plan. You could have written it on a napkin, a very small napkin. And he was teaching sixth grade, an age that people tell me is from hell."

"Math was first on the agenda. There was a short lesson to teach and a worksheet for the kids to complete. Simple enough, huh? It was then that I realized the sound level in the room was approaching that of the Michigan football stadium. Everyone was talking; some were nearly screaming in order to be heard. No one was listening to the lesson. I stopped and stood there quietly. It took about three minutes before anyone realized that no one was teaching. They quieted down and I went on. It stayed quiet for about two minutes. Then the sound of the fury began again. It went on all day."

"About noon my throat began to get sore and I realized that the louder they got, the louder I talked. When I asked a kid for an answer, he/she would whisper it back to me. It was so loud in the room you could barely have heard a cannonball drop. By the time I realized that I had lost control, there was absolutely no getting it back. The natives had taken over the store."

"I would like to tell you that the afternoon was better and, for the first half hour, it was. During that half hour I read from a Harry Potter book. Most of the class paid some attention to the story, but none of them gave it their complete attention. It was like they could not pay attention to anything for more than a minute or two."

"I thought Geography would be a snap. Each student had a big Arizona map that was encased in plastic. All they had to do was answer some pretty simple questions by looking over the map. I even gave them some hints: "What town sounds like a musical instrument and is located north of Phoenix?" I thought it would be a fun lesson. The only problem was, the students didn't want to look for the answers. They wanted someone to tell them the answers."

"Even the grease pencils were a headache. They were the kind you unravel from the top in order to get a sharp point. All had a point when the class began. Five minutes later half of the pencils were broken, unraveled, or both."

"When I looked up at the clock it was 1:50 p.m. and we hadn't done the one-minute math test. The kids rushed to the front to get their individual tests. Because they were all on different numbers, that procedure took a while. Finally they were all settled down with the test in front of them. That one-minute test was the only time there was when I felt I had complete order in my classroom. And that was because they only had one minute to do it and the students who didn't finish the entire test could not hand it in. They had to repeat it the next day. About six kids managed to finish their tests. I secretly smiled to myself as I passed up all the students who didn't finish the test. It was the only victory I had all day."

Jerry

Although Jerry's description of his subbing experience was written with tongue in cheek, I think it is probably typical of what most alternative teachers would experience should they decide to switch gears and enter the teaching profession. Real teaching of real kids is not an easy task. It may sound like fun, but it is an extremely challenging endeavor to undertake at any age. Expecting someone to accept and ultimately enjoy that challenge in his "golden" years - especially without adequate training and preparation – is little more than fantasy.

Now you be the judge. Have our policy makers studied
the ramifications of these laws? Do they honestly believe this
kind of legislation will alleviate the teacher shortage? Do they
think a significant number of competent scientists, doctors,
physicists, or accountants will choose to trade the big bucks of
the private sector for a significantly lower paying teaching
job? How long do they think the alternative licensee will
remain in teaching before becoming disillusioned? Is it wise to
spend bushels of money we don't have on implementing yet
another piece of legislation that is almost certainly doomed to
fail? (For starters, consider the **$35 million** appropriated by
the federal government in the 2002 fiscal year budget for a
"Transition to Teaching" program.)

An attempt to solve our national teacher shortage with
alternative teaching licensing laws is like putting a miniature
band-aid on a four-inch deep bullet wound. It may cover the
hole, but it won't solve the problem.

If we are serious about wanting to provide competent,
trained, dedicated people for our nations' kids, we must bite
the bullet and significantly raise the salaries of teachers. Then,
and only then, will we retain the best of our current teachers
and entice the best and the brightest of our young people to
enter the teaching profession. The $35 million mentioned
earlier would go a long way in raising teachers' salaries.

The kind of world we live in tomorrow depends not partially – but entirely upon the type and quality of the education of our children today.

- Martin Van Bee

20

TRANSFORMING

On September 17, 2001 little Keith Frondle of Cedar Rapids, Iowa died of complications caused by asthma. It was one week before his eleventh birthday. Following Keith's death, his classmates collected $678 to purchase Scooby-Doo books for the school library and Scooby-Doo dolls for local hospital emergency rooms. Why did they choose to honor Keith's memory with Scooby-Doo books and artifacts?

Keith was a longtime Scooby-Doo devotee. He loved that little character – the dolls, the cartoons, and the posters. The thing Keith didn't love was - READING. Keith could read, but he didn't want to read. He was what we call a "reluctant reader." Ironically, one week before Keith's unexpected demise, the school librarian tempted him with four Scooby-Doo books. He read all four of them in the last week of his life! Little Keith Frondle was transformed from a reluctant reader into a ravenous reader within *one* week.

Across the country we have thousands of reluctant readers. Reluctant readers are kids between the ages of 7 and 14 who have learned how to read, but have no desire to read. Most reluctant readers differ from Keith in that they do not become ravenous readers within a one-week timeframe. This transformation normally takes considerably longer, and almost always requires concentrated effort. (One might wonder if a higher power felt the need to rush the timetable for young Keith Frondle.)

Let's pause a moment and reflect on what Mark Twain had to say about reading. He said, "The man who doesn't read good books has no advantage over the man who can't read them." In this chapter we will look at some methods that have proven effective in getting kids to the point where they *do* read because they want to.

Focus on your child's interests.
According to Bonnie Spivack, a Reading Specialist in the Arlington, Virginia Public Schools, a statistic exists that states, "Interest is thirty times more important than reading ability in determining whether a reader will choose to read a selection and then comprehend its contents." Although I question how a statistic such as this could be accurately determined, my experience tells me it is probably true.

If your child is interested in sports, subscribe to one or two sports magazines. If he enjoys the comics, subscribe to a daily newspaper. If he is hooked on stock car racing, purchase a kit (and manual) on "How to Build Your Own Stock Car." If he looks to Kurt Warner as a role model (don't we all?), check out a biography on Kurt from your local library or buy him his own copy as a gift for some special occasion.

You may have noticed I consistently use the pronoun "he" when referring to the reluctant reader. This is not by accident, nor is it intended to be sexist. Normally, boys present more of a challenge than girls do when it comes to motivating a reader. (Of course there are exceptions.)

Boys are less inclined to develop an emotional connection with fiction than girls are. Third and fourth grade girls usually become enthralled with the *Little House on the Prairie* books, and they savor each and every one in the series. And what do their male counterparts do? They struggle through a chapter or two of the first book and decide it is just some "junk" written for a bunch of namby-pamby girls. They don't like it, and they refuse to read it! Amen.

How do we reach these boys that are reluctant to read? Well, we encourage them to read what they want to read rather than what we want them to read. Boys normally prefer non-fiction books. They enjoy reading about nature and science-related topics. They like to read books about their favorite leisure time activities, and the role models associated with those endeavors. For fiction, boys tend to like books with short chapters, humor, suspense, and some slightly gross things that make them feel what they are reading is just a tiny bit perverted.

Allow your son (or male student) to read what he wants, as long as it doesn't cross the boundaries of acceptable behavior. Once he's hooked on reading books that appeal to his taste, you can move him (slowly and gently) into better literature. Remember, you must hook a fish before you reel it in. The hook for the reluctant reader is a topic that interests him.

In order to avoid any misunderstanding, allow me to share one final thought about boys (or girls) choosing their own reading materials. Although adults should not attempt to dictate a child's reading taste, they are obligated to forbid the reading of harmful topics. A child does not need to know how to build a bomb out of items found under the kitchen sink, or understand the demented thinking of a pedophiliac. It is our responsibility to keep damaging reading out of our homes, our schools, and our children's hands.

A particularly good source of information on how to reach struggling male readers can be found on the Internet at www.guysread.com. If you have an unmotivated male reader between the ages of 7 and 14, I highly recommend this site. It contains a wealth of practical and useful suggestions guaranteed to entice the reluctant male reader into the wonderful world of books.

Model reading in your home.
("Model" is a current teacher buzzword. It simply means that you Let-Him-See-You-Do-It.) When your youngster observes you reading, you are sending a subliminal message that says, "READING IS IMPORTANT." Most of us would agree that kids imitate what they *see* more often than what they *hear* (unless it's "naughty" words). Let your kids see you reading on an everyday basis. You do not necessarily *have* to read from a book to accomplish your purpose. A magazine, newspaper, or any printed material will accomplish your purpose. Be aware, however, that optimal benefits are derived when your child observes you reading for pleasure, as well as for information.

You are your child's first teacher, and quite possibly his most influential teacher. When your child sees you reading on a somewhat regular basis, he comes to realize that reading is more than an isolated subject taught in the classroom and graded by a teacher. He eventually internalizes the fact that reading is a requisite for a complete and fulfilling life. The consistent parental practice of modeling reading is more effective than threatening, coaxing, rationalizing, or bribing. (It's also easier on the vocal chords.)

Establish a mandatory, daily reading time in your home.
At this point you're probably thinking, "This lady is out of touch with today's kid. There is no way my child will stand for that regime." Well, he probably won't stand for it. Go ahead and let him sit. This is one of those times when you may need to practice Tough Love. In fact, you probably will have

to practice it if you really and truly want to entice your reluctant reader into the world of books.

There are a few guidelines to keep in mind when you embark on a required daily reading program. Mandatory reading time should not be lengthy. Fifteen minutes is sufficient. The time slot should precede the fun activities, occur at the same time every day (including weekends and summers), and be uninterrupted by telephone calls from friends. ("I'll take your number and he'll return your call in a few minutes.") Exceptions should be granted only for compelling reasons, and only on rare occasions.

Initially, expect your reluctant reader to pout (after he has yelled and gotten nowhere) and just stare at one page for fifteen minutes. But...hang in there. After a few days he will tire from the monotony of just glaring at you (you won't notice) or staring at his book. He'll start to read!

If at all possible, make your child's mandatory reading time a FAMILY READING TIME. It is not realistic (or fair) to expect your reluctant reader to become absorbed in the pages of a book while the rest of the family is hooting and hollering over a favorite TV sit-com. Although this practice may feel uncomfortable and less than enjoyable at the onset, it will improve with time. Try it. I think you'll like it. And if you don't like it, consider it a cost of parenting!

Give a book as a gift.

The simple act of wrapping a book in an appealing manner, and presenting it for a special occasion sends a strong message to your child. It tells him you value reading, and feel its rewards are precious enough to share.

Utilize your Public Library.

Make a weekly library "date" with your young child. Let him browse through books appropriate for his age while you wander through the adult section. You might want top off your "date" with a treat at your youngster's favorite haunt.

Enroll your little one in the public library's summer incentive reading program, and show your support by monitoring his progress.

When your child is old enough to be left alone at the library (before he gets "wheels"), you might want to drop him off while you do your grocery shopping. And when you pick him up – remember the "date" treat!

Encourage your older child to go alone to the library at least once a week for some browsing time. Of course you hope he'll spot a book that intrigues him, and he'll decide to check it out - for that mandatory reading time at home. (You may even want to send along a couple of bucks so that he can pick up his own after-the-library-visit treat.)

Discuss what each family member is reading.

Notice that I said, 'discuss'. This is not synonymous with "quiz." Your goal here is not to determine if your child is actually reading and remembering every detail, but to simply visit about what he is reading and what you are currently reading. Try not to be judgmental. Perhaps your daughter is reading a biography about Britney Spears, and you strongly dislike Ms. Spears. Well, bite your lip. Remember, it's your daughter that you're trying to entice to read. You already know the joy and the satisfaction that comes from losing yourself in a book. If your daughter experiences that pleasure while reading about Britney, then let her be.

Entice your reluctant reader with a read-aloud chapter book.

Over the past six years teachers and parents have hooked thousands of kids into reading through the oral sharing of the Harry Potter books. Kids become enthralled with the storyline and begin to "sneak" a look at the book to see what's coming next. Pick a chapter book that you feel certain will appeal to your reluctant reader and try it at home. (Yes, you can use the mandatory daily reading time for this purpose instead of individual, silent reading.) Remember...your goal is to entice your child to read, and you will be successful in meeting your goal only if you can instill a desire to read. As with most destinations, there are several ways to get there. Pick the path that feels comfortable to you.

Tempt him with a book he can't refuse.

An excellent resource for helping you find just the right book is the *Best Books for Kids Who Think They Hate to Read,* by Laura Backes. It is available at most public libraries, major bookstores, and on the Web. The book examines 125 different books that "will turn any child (7-14) into a lifelong reader." Each book review includes a picture of the cover, the genre (mystery, romance, science-fiction, etc.), the suggested reading level, number of pages, a synopsis of the main idea, a short excerpt, and the type of child that it will appeal to. Teachers and parents alike will find this book extremely beneficial in determining which books will appeal to kids with varying personalities, skill levels, and interests.

When I was very young, I often lamented to my mother that I would probably never find "Mr. Right." Her rebuttal to my verbalized concern never varied. She consistently said, "Oh yes you will. There's a lid for every pot and a frame for every picture." I believe she could have added, "...and a book for every kid." It's up to us to find that special book that will make our reluctant reader *want* to read.

Appeal to his vanity.

Every child likes to see his name or picture in the newspaper. Do you think he would be thrilled (and motivated to read another book) if he saw his own book review and *his* name posted on the World Wide Web? Ah, yes. There's no doubt about it! Book Nook is a web site where kids are allowed (and encouraged) to write book reviews. After your child (any age) has completed a book, assist him in locating the web site at http://I-site.on.ca/booknook.html. Once at the site he can write a review of his book, post it, and then wait for it to appear along with his name. Of course grandpas, grandmas, aunts, uncles, cousins and neighbors should be alerted to this monumental achievement. (It's okay to drop a hint to the plumber and the mailman, too.) It's a pretty safe bet that all "interested parties" will reward your budding reader with some encouraging words. And what's the ultimate payoff? Your reluctant reader will choose to read another book and write another book review! Success is almost always followed with even greater effort, and to a kid - "unsolicited" praise is a sign of success. (Come to think of it, unsolicited praise feels pretty good to adults too. Wouldn't you agree?)

At a teacher's conference some years ago, a noted children's author said this about reading. "The more you read, the better you get. The better you get, the more you read." We must entice our kids to "read more" so that they will "read better", and then choose to read even more.

There is an old Chinese proverb that says, "Your skills will accomplish what the force of many cannot." I believe this is true when we think of the reluctant reader and the parent. The love, the modeling, and the concern of a parent can accomplish what the force of many teachers cannot.

Teach your children a love of reading and you have given them a most precious gift.

- Roger Lewin

21

THE ABC's OF HOMEWORK

This chapter calls for some interaction on your part, so limber up those muscles. I want you to wave both hands wildly in the air if you find the next statement applicable to your household. **"When I invite my child to sit with me so we can work on a school skill that is causing him difficulty, he always responds with a shout of joy and breaks into a huge smile."** Mmm. My mental telepathy doesn't show much waving. As a matter of fact, I don't even sense a single finger lifting from the page.

Okay, one more chance. If this next statement applies to you, scream out in your loudest voice, "YIPPEE, THAT'S ME!" **"I have lots of extra time on my hands to help my kids with the skills they need to practice."**(I can't hear you!)

Your lack of response suggests you have a typical family. Kids normally don't WANT to sit down and "practice" anything. Furthermore, most parents have difficulty finding the time to initiate and supervise the practice of a skill or the completion of homework.

"Homework" for the young child often consists of practicing a particular skill that has been presented at school, but not yet mastered. Keeping in mind the fact that KIDS LEARN EVERYTHING MORE QUICKLY WHEN IT IS TAUGHT OR PRACTICED IN A GAME FORMAT, I would like to share with you some ideas that have worked for me in the classroom. You may want to try them with your child. I guarantee your little one will solidify some concepts and increase some skills by participating in these games. Better still, he'll have fun and so will you.

The "games" I am suggesting are ones that you can play while simultaneously doing other chores, or riding in the car. The activities are geared primarily to the child between ages four and nine. However, many can be modified and used with the older child as well. Once you get the basic idea of taking the "ill" out of dr<u>ill</u>, your own creative ideas will emerge and you'll find the variations endless.

Pre-reading and Early Reading Skills:

If your child can rhyme and knows his beginning consonant sounds, he is on his way to becoming an independent reader. When he learns to read the word "cat", he automatically will recognize *bat, fat,* and *hat*.

RHYMING:

Identifying words that rhyme (by sound – not sight), and thinking of a word that rhymes with another word, are two very important pre-reading skills. Games can be played to develop these skills as early as age three. (Kids are never too old to profit from these games if the format is enjoyable and the atmosphere is free of stress.)

- Recite a few of your favorite nursery rhymes that *you* enjoyed as a child. When one appears to "click" with your youngster, repeat it. Invite your little one to join in. If you still have his interest, invite him to play, <u>You Fill In The Missing Word</u>. "Jack and Jill went up the _____, to fetch a pail of _____." Next, play <u>Every Other Line</u>. You say the first line and your child says the next. Reverse the order. And finally, invite your child to say the rhyme 'all by himself.' Remember to praise **all** attempts.

- <u>I'm Thinking Of A Word</u>. "I'm thinking of a word that is in the sky and rhymes with *car*."

- <u>Which Two Words Rhyme</u>? "Bus, toy, fuss."

BEGINNING AND ENDING CONSONANT SOUNDS:
Games designed for practicing beginning and ending consonant sounds are most effective when they are introduced <u>after</u> the concept of rhyming is mastered. (It is important to use the terms *rhyme* and *beginning sound* as often as possible. Children need to learn that these two terms are not synonymous.)

- <u>Can You Find...</u>? "Can you find something in the kitchen that <u>starts</u> with the letter *m*?" Go to the family room and look for something that <u>ends</u> with *n*." (It is best to work with ending sounds *after* the child has fully mastered the beginning sound concept.)

- <u>Can You Think Of A Word</u>? "Can you think of an animal's name that starts with *s*?" "Can you think of a vegetable that starts with the letter *c*? For variation, let your child supply the question and you give the answer.

- <u>I'll Say The Word, You Tell Me The Letter</u> (that the word begins or ends with). "MOTHER"_____ "HAT"_____. Remember to let your little one have some turns at being "teacher."

- <u>How Many Words?</u> "How many words can you think of that start with *t*? You say the words and I'll count." Later you can suggest he does the counting as you give your list of words. (That might be called, "Killing Two Birds With One Stone.") Nah, I'm just kidding.

Number Skills:

COUNTING OBJECTS: When your child is learning to count, it is extremely important that he <u>touch</u> each item as he counts. This process is called one-to-one correspondence, and is much more beneficial than the simple memory task of saying the numbers from one to ten. (The child does not need to learn the "one-to-one correspondence" terminology – only the concept.)

- <u>Can You Help Me?</u> "Can you please tell me how many items are in the green clothesbasket so I will know if this load will fit in the washer?" Or, "Please count out five spoons, forks, and knives and put them on the table for me."

NUMERAL RECOGNITION: Time is well spent when you provide opportunities for your child to practice recognizing numbers on an informal basis. When you get in the "watch for numbers" mindset, you'll be amazed at how many you have in your home. The calendar, TV, microwave, VCR, scales, clock, and stove are a few that come to mind. There are many more.

- <u>What Number Is It?</u> "What numbers are showing on the digital clock right now?" "Please punch in number 7 on the remote control." "What number is showing on the microwave?" "Point to the number on the calendar

that tells us the day we're going to Grandma's house."
"What channel is the TV turned to?" Riding in the car
provides dozens of variations for this game.

COINS: Coin activities allow for a variety of math
experiences that provide a vast array of benefits. Some of the
important skills gained through playing with coins include
seeing likenesses and differences, categorizing, counting with
one-to-one correspondence, and coin recognition. The more
advanced skills of learning coin values and determining totals
are learned much easier and more quickly if the child has had
ample opportunity to manipulate and handle *real* coins.
(Avoid using cardboard or plastic look-alike coins. They are
not nearly as effective as the real thing.)

- Funny Money. "While I fold the clothes, I'd like you
  to empty the change from my purse and dump it on the
  floor. Sort all the coins that look alike into different
  piles. Count the nickels. Make the pennies form a
  circle. Arrange the dimes in a square." Caution. Kids
  cannot accomplish ALL of this on a first, second, or
  even third try. Start with the simplest tasks and look
  for mastery before moving on to the more difficult
  areas. Advanced skills might involve questions such
  as, "How much money do I have in dimes? What is the
  total amount of money in my pocket today?" ("Not
  enough", might be your answer. Your child needs to be
  more exact.)

MATH FACTS: These games can be played with addition, subtraction, multiplication, or division.

- In the early stages, I like to start with, <u>You Be The Teacher</u>. "You give me the problem, I'll give you the answer." Your child says, "Four plus two," and you supply the answer.

- Reverse the above procedure and call it, <u>My Turn</u>. "This time I'll say the problem and you give *me* the answer."

- Kids love to play <u>Caught-Cha</u>. The parent says, "I'll give you a problem *and* the answer. If my answer is correct, you say "Right." If my answer is incorrect, you **yell** "Caught-Cha." Reverse roles.

SPELLING: Oral spelling practice is much more fun for kids than written practice is. It is equally as beneficial.

- This game is called, <u>Taking Turns</u>. "Let's take turns spelling your word list. I'll say the first word and spell it. Then I'll say the next word and *you* spell it." Reverse the procedure.

- Most kids enjoy playing <u>Every Other Letter</u>. "I'll start by saying the word and the first letter. You say the next letter and we'll continue taking turns." Reverse the procedure by letting your child start.

Hopefully, these ideas will inspire you to take the **ill** out of **drill** in order to increase your child's **skill.** I urge you to try it because I think you'll like it. I know your child will. Best of all, your youngster will be learning while he *thinks* he is playing.

Homework for the older child is considerably more complicated and demanding than it is for the little guy. (Duh!) Perhaps some of these complaints sound familiar.

"Jack won't do his homework unless I'm sitting right with him, pushing him every step of the way."

"I know Josie can do it on her own, but she won't! I end up doing a lot (or all) of it and I know that's wrong. But if I don't do it, it won't get done."

"Mason hides his homework from us, then tells us he's done it when he hasn't!"

"Angie does nothing in class, brings her unfinished work home, and then we work on it together until all hours of the night. I've had it!"

If any of this sounds like you talking, take comfort. You have a lot of companions. "Experts" estimate that in any given classroom, there are at least five kids who can't be trusted to do their homework on their own. (I don't claim to be an expert, but I think five may be on the low end of reality). At home, you must "stand over her" or the homework doesn't get done. At school, the teacher also has to "stand over her" or the class work isn't completed.

So why do parents and teachers do this? Because we don't want kids to "fail", that's why! Our motive is commendable. But, does it foster responsibility and independence? Perhaps we need to do some introspection so we can honestly and effectively evaluate our attitudes and policies regarding homework.

Are we really teaching our kids the skills of responsibility, perseverance, and time management when we constantly question them about their homework assignments? Probably not. Are we promoting initiative, self-reliance and resourcefulness when we harangue them about what they have to do and when it is supposed to be done? I doubt it. Are these emotional and behavioral skills really necessary in order to successfully meet the demands of adult life? Ah, yes – no doubt about that one! Is it easy to break old habits even if they aren't working? No, it absolutely and positively is not.

At this point I can sense your impatience. You're thinking, "Yada, yada, I know what the problem is. What's the solution?"

The "solution" as I perceive it, comes from someone who has had far more experience working with older students than I have. (He also has a lot more initials after his name.) I am referring to family psychologist and nationally recognized parenting authority, Dr. John Rosemond. (Yup, the same one I'm at odds with concerning the percentage of kids taking Ritalin.) You may be familiar with Dr. Rosemond's syndicated columns. They appear in over 100 Knight-Ridder newspapers and in *Better Homes and Gardens.*

In his book, ENDING THE HOMEWORK HASSLE, Dr. Rosemond has a section called "The ABC's of Effective Homework Management." His recommendations are considerably different from the advice of many other so-called experts. I suspect his recommended practices also differ from the methods you may have tried.

If your "homework cop" policy has been unsuccessful, you may want to try Dr. Rosemond's suggestions. They make sense to me, and I hope they will be helpful to you. (Of course, if your homework methods "ain't" broken, they don't need fixin'.) If that's the case, you can skip the next few pages and proceed to Chapter 22. Although I have paraphrased the following suggestions, and added a few "gems" of my own, the credit for the ideas (and captions) goes to Dr. Rosemond.

"A" STANDS FOR "ALL BY MYSELF." The child should do his homework in a private place, preferably at a desk in his room. He will be less distracted if he is not working in a family gathering area. It is your responsibility to see that your child's bedroom (or study area) is "self-contained." In other words, it should be stocked with everything he will need in order to do his homework. This plan means that he completes his homework on his own. It eliminates excuses for venturing out of his cozy little study area for the purported purpose of getting "supplies." Incidentally, he does not need a TV or a telephone in his room. Furthermore, make the computer off limits during this time, unless it is needed to complete the assignment.

"B" STANDS FOR "BACK OFF." This means you stay out of your child's homework unless you are asked to get involved. It means you do not ask questions like, "Do you need any help with your homework"? "How can you do homework with that music playing?" "Do you have any homework today?"

Dr. Rosemond suggests you not do any checking to see if your guidelines are being followed. I, however, am a bit

165

skeptical about that advice. It seems to me that an occasional peek couldn't hurt too much. Perhaps each parent must decide for himself which plan of action he believes would be most effective for his child. (No, I'm not "straddling the fence." I'm simply offering two options that reflect a difference in opinion.)

Don't provide the child with a shortcut. This means you do not (under any circumstances) do your child's work for him. If he complains he can't do it on his own, suggest he ask his teacher to explain it a second time or give him some extra help before or after school. Of course you are implying that your child is responsible for his own learning and he needs to pay closer attention in class. You are also insinuating that if he is unwilling to accept this responsibility, he had better get prepared to suffer the consequences.

Don't get in over your head. If your child brings work to you for help and it looks like "Greek", don't bang your head against the book trying to learn the subject matter. Again, this is an appropriate time to refer your child back to his teacher.

Don't get involved in an emotional tussle over homework. If your child complains (and he will) that you aren't explaining it "right" or that your method isn't like Mrs. Smith's is, butt out! Simply say, "Well I guess I'm not the one to help you then." Excuse yourself and leave the room. ALLOW NO SECOND CHANCES (that night). It's amazing how motivating a refusal can be when at some later date your youngster might request assistance! (He's not going to repeat his mistake of complaining about your help when he's had to suffer a consequence - no siree!)

"C" STANDS FOR "CALL IT QUITS AT A REASONABLE HOUR." Set an upper time limit on homework. Usually, a child can decide when to <u>start</u> his homework. (The parent should NEVER give him more than one reminder.) The parent, however, must set a nonnegotiable deadline to quit. And what if his homework isn't done? Then he will have to suffer the consequences. Next time he'll start earlier, or have to suffer the consequences again! The third time is usually the charm.

Granted, all of this stuff might sound like too much "tough love" for you to swallow. I readily admit that it is not an easy plan. If your child has already succeeded in getting you involved in the "homework trap", a major change will take time. When you first initiate your "transfer of responsibility" plan, you can expect a period of three to four weeks to elapse before you see the fruits of your labor. You can also expect your child's homework responsibilities to worsen at first, and then gradually improve. Why?

Initially your child will revel in the fact that you are not constantly hounding him about his homework, and he will probably take a self-imposed holiday from his "drudgery." However, after "consequence time" comes around (e.g. a parent-imposed one or the next report card), your child will probably improve his homework habits on his own volition.

Before leaving the topic of homework, I would like to add a few thoughts about consequences. The first consequence of homework habits and responsibility appears in the form of a grade that is issued by the teacher. The parent should not "go to bat" for the child by contacting the teacher in an attempt to raise a grade. If teacher contact is necessary (and it very well might be), the student should be forced to accompany the parent to the conference. Such a plan insures that all concerned parties are on the same page. It also places the primary responsibility for completed homework directly where it should be – in the hands of the student.

I have one final caution concerning parental consequences that accompany any misdeed – including uncompleted or poorly done homework. First and foremost, you need to remember that you are not engaged in a popularity contest. If you have resorted to a threat of any kind (no sleepovers, take-away-the-car, quit your job, etc.), you must enforce it if your child does not meet his obligations. To do otherwise is a disservice to your child.

It is also important for you to remind yourself that if you choose to implement the "**You** Take the Responsibility" plan, it is in your child's best interest. Yes, your offspring may take some lumps in the form of lower marks for a time, and he will most definitely risk the teacher's displeasure. However, all of us learn from our mistakes. You should not rob your child of the opportunity to learn from his mistakes. You are giving your child a gift by teaching him responsibility, perseverance, time management, initiative, self-reliance and resourcefulness. It is a gift of priceless value, and it will serve him well.

Few things help an individual more than to place responsibility upon him, and to let him know that you trust him.

- *Booker T. Washington*

22

WELL BULLY FOR YOU

In the last chapter I asked for some verbal feedback. Now I have a mental exercise I would like you to participate in. I want you to think w-a-a-a-y back. When you were growing up, did you have a bully in your class, your neighborhood, your park, your playground, or in your *family*? Sure you did! Bullies have always been around. Bullying, however, is much more prevalent and serious today than it was even fifteen years ago.

Bullying is displayed through an inequality of power, and involves one person having "fun" at another's expense. **Bullying in its extreme form is an act of terrorism**. If you think that statement is an exaggeration, take a look at the FBI's definition of terrorism. The FBI defines terrorism as an "unlawful use of force or violence against persons or property to intimidate or coerce..." The hardcore bully is a terrorist!

Bullies come in different sizes, ages, shapes, and colors. In the past, most bullies were male. In the early nineties a significant number of females joined the Bully Brigade. (If you doubt this, ask any middle or high school teacher or check the rolls of the penal institutions for women.) Although bullies look different and exercise their power in different ways, they share several commonalities.

All bullies feel the need to control others. Bullies exercise their power on younger, smaller, or emotionally weaker victims. Bullies have low self-esteem that they attempt to cover up through their intimidation of others. They constantly try to convince themselves (and demonstrate to others) that they are superior, and their victims are "losers."

Oftentimes a bully has been a victim of bullying during his formative years. The perpetrator has most likely been an adult relative (often a parent), or an older sibling. The bullying may have been in the form of excessive, unrelenting tickling or intimidating, coercive verbal abuse. The child who has been subjected to extreme physical abuse in the home <u>rarely</u> becomes a bully. The victim of hardcore physical treatment is more likely to retreat within himself because he has been made to feel unworthy of normal, caring treatment from others. It is more likely he will become the victim of peer bullying, rather than the perpetrator.

Bullying is enacted in one of three ways. It can be in the form of verbal abuse. ("You're too stupid to fight your way out of a paper bag."). It might be emotional abuse. ("No wonder you're never invited to a party. You're freakin' WIERD!"). And the abuse most commonly associated with bullying - physical threats or the act itself. ("Give me your lunch money or I'll beat you to a pulp.")

In the past, girls normally engaged in verbal and emotional bullying and boys resorted to physical violence. Today, that line of demarcation is much cloudier. Both genders have been observed inflicting all three forms of bullying.

Bullying of any kind causes pain for the victim. The suffering can be in the form of realistic fear for one's safety, or in feelings of unworthiness. Either way, the pain is real and destructive. Each time a child is forced to suffer the power of a bully, the wound becomes deeper and the scar lasts longer.

Some believe that the victim of a bully never fully forgets the pain, the humiliation, and the fear caused by the perpetrator. Adults who have suffered from childhood bullying often concur with this assessment. More often than not, the wounded kid grows up to be a wounded adult.

If we are going to avoid a society of wounded adults, we must first attempt to help our wounded kids – the ones who are victims of a bully. As teachers, parents, principals, coaches, Scout leaders, the clergy, and yes – neighbors, it is up to us to do all we can to prevent kids from being bullied. We must also be realistic and acknowledge the fact that we will never be one hundred percent effective in our prevention endeavors. Consequently, we need to be prepared to help our children cope if they do become the target of a bully.

One of the first things a bullied child must deal with is determining when it is appropriate to tell an adult, and when it is not. A child under eight often reports any and every perceived injustice to a teacher or parent. When he is older, he usually doesn't report bullying for the fear of being labeled a tattletale.

A common tattling guideline taught by most school counselors is one that can also be used effectively in the home. The guideline (with some variations) sounds like this. "If another person (child or adult) has physically hurt you, threatened you, or touched you in an inappropriate manner, you must report it IMMEDIATELY to a trusted adult. If, however, the unsettling episode is an isolated incident and consists primarily of teasing ("You don't know how to *what*?"), or name calling ("Hey, scary Mary"), you should first try to handle the situation yourself. Remember to use the problem-solving skills we have practiced. If your solution doesn't work, then you should ask an adult for help."

Now let's pretend your child has just arrived home from school, clearly upset. He is attempting to report (between sobs) his version of some bullying incident. What might you do?

First of all, suppress your initial reaction to beat the offender within an inch of his life. (An assault and battery charge doesn't send a very good message to your kid.) Next, listen to your child's story. Keep in mind that when you listen, you don't talk. You do not pry for details (at this point), and you don't offer solutions. You simply listen as your child "unloads." You are in effect, being an "emotional coach" to your child when you encourage him to talk about his problems and his feelings.

Next, you empathize. You do this by letting your child know that you understand how he is feeling (no matter how trivial the incident may seem to you). A statement like, "I can imagine how scared (hurt, angry, embarrassed) you must have been," tells your child that his feelings are being validated. In other words, he knows that you understand he is feeling lower than a snake's belly and you feel badly for him.

Your next action depends on the severity of the problem as you see it. If the bullying was to the extent that it left any kind of mark on your child's body or clothing (excluding rips caused accidentally while playing tag or some similar game,) you immediately do two things. Take a photo of the "evidence" and make a list of all details of the incident. Restrict your list to the facts as they are reported to you. Do not list your feelings, your solutions, or your ideas of punishment for the offender. Next, with list in hand, go to the adult(s) in charge of the area where the offense allegedly occurred. If the bullying happened on the bus, go to the bus driver. If it occurred in the classroom, contact the teacher. Listen to the adult's perception of the incident, and solicit his help.

If the bullying has taken place in the neighborhood or in some other unsupervised area, you must approach the bully's parent and discuss the situation. This is not a pleasant task, nor an easy one. But, your obligation as a parent is to protect your child above all else. If it costs you a "friendship" – so be it.

It is never a good idea for a parent to approach a child bully about his actions, in the absence of the bully's parent. That situation gives the bully a golden opportunity to report untruths about the manner in which he was confronted. Furthermore, it often gives him an incentive to intensify his crummy treatment toward his victim – your child.

In all cases of bullying (no matter where the offense happens) it is wise to notify your child's teacher and your school's principal. They need to be informed about what has happened so they can help your child work through the situation, and be alert for possible future incidents. Schools are mandated to protect kids from violence, and they take that responsibility *very* seriously. You enable them to help when you notify them of a bullying incident, and share the details.

Before moving on, I want to share a common myth that I hope you will not buy into. The myth says, "**If you don't want to be bullied, just ignore it.**" Be aware that most children do not have the ability to ignore bullying. Furthermore, their futile attempts at trying to do so often causes the bullying to intensify. Bullies do not give up easily. Although a few "experts" continue to offer the "ignore it" advice, I urge you not to accept it. It is a platitude that sounds sensible, but one that seldom works.

Although teasing is a milder form of bullying, it still creates stress and causes pain for the victim. A common form of teasing that many young children are faced with is the unwelcome invitation to "play." The complaint sounds something like this. "I don't want to go outside for recess. Johnny is always chasing me on the playground and I HATE it." This type of complaint deserves to be addressed, but it usually can be dealt with in the home. It seldom requires outside intervention.

When your child complains about being teased, you need to listen and empathize the same as you would if the bullying were physical. After that, some changes are in order. Write down a list of possible solutions (even the ridiculous ones) that your child suggests might work. Go over each solution and discuss the consequences. Together, cross out the "bad" ideas. At this point you may need to suggest another solution, if there is an obvious one that your child has failed to think of.

When you and your child have agreed on a possible solution, try acting it out. We call this "role playing." You can play the bully, and your child can practice his solution. Reverse the roles. Kids love this activity, and more importantly -they learn from it. Allow me to share with you an example of some role-playing that I used many times following a "Johnny is chasing me" complaint.

I would say, "Let's pretend you are Johnny and I'll be you. You go over to the swings and then run at me as fast as you can yelling, 'I'm going to chase you.'" Of course the child would comply. I would stand in my original spot and not move a muscle. When the kid got nose to belt buckle level, he invariably said – "But you're supposed to run." To which I would reply, "But I don't want to run. And if I don't run, you can't chase me." It worked every time!

Often times a solution to a teasing problem is relatively simple. Kids simply need an adult's guidance to help them see what the solution is. It is their right to receive that assistance, and it is our obligation to give it.

No matter how severe or how slight the bullying might be, it is vitally important that the victim be made to understand that it is the bully's behavior that is wrong. A victim must be reassured (repeatedly) that he is not inferior in any way, and he is not the cause of the problem. A bully's mean behavior indicates the bully has a problem within himself. The victim is simply a convenient target.

Now I would like you to recall the opening paragraph where I mentioned the different places kids encounter bullies. I referred to the town, school, playground, neighborhood, and even the household. Sometimes we tend to overlook the fact that bullies come from families, just like victims do. And, just as victims need extra help and guidance, so do perpetrators. Help for the bully is considerably different than it is for victims, but it is certainly no less important. The parent that denies his child's bullying or refuses to address it, is destined to see a dysfunctional adult sitting at his Christmas dinner table. It is a guarantee that comes without exceptions.

Parents normally become aware of their child being mean to others in one of two ways, and neither is pleasant. One is the humiliating, dreaded, bad-news phone call from the teacher. It usually sounds something like this.

"I think you need to know that for some time your son, Jake, has been taunting his classmates about things he sees as imperfections. Today in the lunchroom Jake bit the girl sitting next to him and called her a 'stupid boobycakes'. I think we need to talk."

Boom! The bubble has burst. Your kid is not perfect, and you're being asked to deal with it.

Another way of learning about your child's bullying behavior happens when you overhear or see it yourself. You hear a commotion in the backyard and go to the window to see what is going on. Peering out with disbelieving eyes, you observe your older son, Jim, chasing his little brother with a steel pipe. He is yelling, "I'm going to KILL you for riding my bike without my permission." Boom, again! This is almost worse than the teacher's call because you can't even rationalize that there must be a mistake. You know what you saw, and you know what you heard.

Initial awareness of a bullying incident is tough on a parent. It's hard to accept that our own precious offspring is capable of inflicting pain through malicious teasing, inhibiting threats, or physical force. But when it happens, we need to acknowledge it and deal with it – immediately! There is no justification for waiting to see if the incident, or something similar, will be repeated. Besides, it's probably not the first offense. It's simply the first time you became aware of it.

When you approach your child about his bullying behavior, take off your kid gloves. Inform him in no uncertain terms that such behavior is totally unacceptable, and will NOT be tolerated. Discuss with him the motives that resulted in his unacceptable behavior, but refuse to accept excuses.

Incidentally, when you are looking for an answer as to *why* he resorted to such reprehensible behavior, be prepared to hear, "I don't know why." That is a universal kid response, and to a certain degree it's probably true. Kids often react without forethought, afterthought, or comprehension of motive. They really don't know why they acted as they did.

After your bully-child has abandoned his pleas for leniency and you have cooled down to room temperature, you need to help him formulate a plan for more acceptable behavior. Help him develop a list of alternative methods that he might use when he is angry, upset, or feeling mean-spirited. Conclude your discussion by naming an unpleasant consequence that will be imposed if the bullying behavior is repeated.

Will the bullying behavior happen again? Yes, it probably will. It would be extremely rare to have any type of negative behavior "cured" with only one discussion and a threat of punishment. So be on the safe side, and expect it to happen.

When (or if) it does, repeat the previous outlined plan, and enforce the disciplinary measure you initially presented. If you fail to enforce your prescribed consequence, you send a message to your child that suggests you don't really feel very strongly about the issue at hand.

A list of appropriate consequences is almost endless, and no doubt you have effective ideas of your own. A few you might want to consider include a week's restriction from the computer, loss of telephone privileges, missing Friday night's football game, or a week without television.

There are four things to keep in mind when you impose a consequence (for *any* kind of misbehavior):

- It should be unpleasant

- It should have a reasonable "stopping" point (forever isn't an option)

- There should be no "Time Off For Good Behavior"

- IT MUST BE ENFORCED

As a mother, I never had to deal with the BULLY issue, but I had numerous other occasions when I was forced to "modify a behavior." (A parent who says he has not had to deal with some kind of "behavior molding" is either being untruthful or suffering from memory loss.) Did I always abide by the consequence guidelines? Nope, I'm afraid not. Does that mean I was a "bad" parent? I don't think so. Every parent slips up now and then. When it happens, we don't need to put on the guilt coat or wring our hands in despair. We need only remind ourselves to try harder next time. A few parental failures do not ruin a child. They just signify our humanness.

Jacquie McTaggart

Now let's look at what you need to do if you have dealt with the bullying issue and your efforts have been unsuccessful. If you have been made aware of three or more incidents when your child has bullied another, it's high time to get the school involved. Make an appointment with your child's teacher(s) and go prepared with a list of questions. It might help to write them down so that "in the heat of passion" you don't forget something you need to know. Your list might look like this:

Is my child being mean to just one kid or several? Is he retaliating to a perceived slight, or is he initiating the mean behavior? Does my child's bullying occur at one specific time of the day (like just before lunch), at one particular location (maybe the playground), or is it usually a random act of meanness? Do you feel that his bullying behavior is in any way connected to an academic problem (either real, or my child's perception of one)? How have you and/or the principal dealt with my child's behavior? What suggestions do you have for me?

Develop a plan with the teacher that spells out three things.

- The behaviors that will be treated as bullying

- The consequence (at school and at home) for future bullying behavior

- The plan for informing you about any future bullying behavior

At the conclusion of the parent-teacher visit, request a joint teacher-parent-student conference for a mutually convenient time. At this meeting the three of you (four, if both parents can attend) can go over the ground-rules together. This assures that all parties involved are on the same page. It also is a powerful prevention for misunderstandings and erroneous excuses.

Caution. Oftentimes a parent will ask the teacher to write a note home every Friday reporting on how the week went. A plan such as this works reasonably well until a particularly hectic Friday when teacher forgets to write the note. Oops. The parent gets upset. Or the teacher has five students on behavior modification plans and all parents have requested weekly updates. She runs out of time and doesn't get all of them written. Oops, again. Or perhaps she wrote the behavior update during her (20 minute) Friday lunch period, and then forgot to give it to your youngster. One more Oops! No matter what the reason is, most parents are understandably unhappy when Friday notes are in the PLAN, but no note is in the bag. When this situation occurs, the parent-teacher relationship erodes and the child ends up suffering the after-effects.

If it is at all possible, try to make a plan with the teacher that will ensure regular communication without the requirement of a weekly written anecdotal report. This might be as simple as a prearranged weekly telephone call, or a quick stop in the classroom before or after school.

Although most problems of bullying can be solved when parents and school work together, that is not always the case. If your efforts fail to eliminate or drastically reduce your child's bullying behavior, (particularly if it is the physical kind) you need to seek professional help. The school counselor is an appropriate place to start. He may, or may not, advise you to consult with a child psychologist. If he does suggest that route, he can provide you with a list of psychologists that he feels are highly competent in their field.

Don't be afraid to solicit continued help from your school counselor and your child's teacher as you work your way through this problem. That is part of their job, and they will help in every way possible.

The true bully rarely outgrows his mean behaviors without intervention and help from adults. It only makes sense to start sooner rather than later. Furthermore, you'll be saving your child, your child's potential victims, and yourself a whole bunch of pain!

You cannot shake hands with a clenched fist.

- Indira

23

RUBBER BANDS

Have you ever wondered why your toddler asks what there is to do, and you need a bulldozer in order to get from his playroom doorway to the toy chest? Or have you been puzzled by your high school kid's complaint about how boring your town is? He complains that there is nothing to do and no place to go.

I used to hear these complaints from my sons and from my students. Now I hear the same grievances from my grandkids. (Some things never change.) I have a theory as to why kids can't think of anything to do, and I'd like to share it with you.

By allowing (and sometimes encouraging) our kids to become over-scheduled, we have made them incapable of the seemingly simple task of figuring out how they can fill their "free" time. Through our acceptance of the call-Susie, play-this, read-that, make-the-team, take-some-lessons, join-the-club mindset, we have robbed kids of the opportunity to plan their own free time.

We decide what they should do and whom they should do it with - every waking minute of their day. When we are busy with tasks around the home, we use the TV, video games, and the computer as electronic babysitters. We arrange "Play Dates" and host "Play Groups" so that our kids can practice their social skills by doing whatever it is that *we* have determined they should do. We spend a week's wage to host the neighborhood's most elaborate birthday party, and we delay our family vacation so that our wee one won't have to miss another child's party. We take our toddlers to Library Hour, and we sign them up for one or two "enrichment" opportunities that are available in the community. When they enter kindergarten, we enroll them in every after school activity, club, or lesson known to man.

As they proceed through the grades, we encourage, demand, or allow them to become involved in all extra-curricular activities offered. The bottom line is this: When we fail to set limits regarding the amount of time our kids engage in extra-curricular activities, we do them a disservice.

Why do we do all of this nonsense? Is it because we want them "out of our hair?" Of course not. There are two reasons most of us buy into this hyper-parenting trap, and they are both products of good intentions. Number one, we have fooled ourselves into believing that an active involvement in a wide range of activities will increase our child's chances for becoming a happy and successful adult. Secondly, we want our kids to have all of the advantages that we didn't have when we were growing up. (I wonder why we feel that way. Most of us are moderately successful at our occupation or vocation, and the majority of us enjoy a modest degree of happiness. Why do we want more for our kids?)

Although these are the rationalizations that we admit to, I suspect there are a couple of less honorable motives that may be lurking someplace within our subconscious. Today, the majority of parents work outside the home so that they can pay the never-ending bills and those pesky taxes (the ones that support our schools). They don't have a lot of time to spend with their kids and they feel guilty. They attempt to ease their guilt and compensate for their lack of involvement in their kids' lives by offering them "special" opportunities.

The second reason is hardly ever admitted – certainly not to others, and possibly not to one's self. It is the parent's desire to see his child as part of the movers and shakers crowd! The parent believes that his super-involved child will most certainly be emulated by all, and envied by most. That kind of parent can almost hear the cheering that will surely happen when his daughter is named Homecoming Queen, or his son is picked to be the captain of the football team. He can hardly wait. He'll send his kid to every camp available, drive to five thousand practices, and pay huge participation fees - just to hear those cheers.

Parents are unwittingly programming and pressuring their kids into being mini-adults. Subconsciously, they are attempting to control everything in their child's environment with the expectation of a perfect outcome. Although the intentions may be laudable, the anticipated outcome is not realistic. Numerous studies have determined **there is no correlation between an adult's success in life and the number of organized activities he engaged in during his formative years**.

Over-scheduling our children is not a recent phenomenon in our society. Forty years ago gregarious high school kids (especially in small, rural communities) were involved in every extra-curricular activity that was offered. Twenty years later, the movement could be seen at the middle school level where it was not at all unusual for a student to be active in three or more sports, vocal music, band, a youth church group, and so on. Another ten years brought it to the elementary level with wrestling clubs, religion classes, gymnastics, Brownies, Clover Kids, tap-dance, 4-H, and ... This craziness has now reached our toddlers and infants with programs such as Swimming for Babes, Kindermusik, Kindergym, Library Hour, Play Dates, and organized Play Groups.

I can almost imagine the next step. Twenty expectant mothers will lie in a circle on the floor with inter-connecting speakers attached to their bellies and plugged into a central DVD player. The unborn children will be able to bond with their fellow fetuses as they listen together to the melodies of Bach and Mozart. Ah, won't it be wonderful? They will really have a head start at developing their social skills. That will of course enhance their chances at being accepted as part of the "IN" crowd, which will ultimately result in lots of that tumultuous cheering! Ridiculous, you say? (I hope I'll still be around to say, "I TOLD YOU SO.")

Individually, all of the above activities –and others not listed - are worthwhile and valuable. (Ignore the expectant mom business. That was just Science Fiction.) They each provide something positive for our kids and they all merit at least some consideration when making, or guiding our kids to make, "free-time" choices. Now reread that last sentence, and take special note of the word choices. That means, "pick and choose." It does NOT mean, "select everything."

We should not encourage, demand, or allow our child to pick every age-appropriate activity that is available within the community. There are far more opportunities available than any one child can or should be involved in. We need to guide him toward the one or two pursuits that he is most interested in.

Oftentimes a parent encourages his child to sample every selection on the activity menu so that he can ultimately pick one or two favorites. Although that sounds like a logical plan, it isn't a very wise one. It stretches the kid too far and leaves him virtually no time to simply be a kid. He loses the opportunity to choose how he wants to spend his leisure time because he's too busy "tasting" the options. Parents need to put their desire to "have-their-kid-revered" on the back burner, and then turn off the stove. It's also a time when they should flex their parental muscles and tell that outgoing, want-to-do-everything-kid, "No!"

If the child demands a reason (and he probably will), the parent is justified in saying that he simply does not think it is wise to spend all free time in scheduled, organized activities. It might smooth a few of the ruffled feathers if the parent explains that he likes to be with his child more than he likes to watch him. (Nobody ever said parenting was easy!)

A parent's task of setting limits on scheduled activities can be less painful if he keeps in mind the fact that in order to thrive, A KID MUST HAVE "DOWN TIME." He needs that time in order to discover who he is and what he enjoys doing, without an adult making up the rules. Perhaps he will choose to simply lie out on the grass and watch the clouds roll by. Or maybe he'll call his friends and organize a puppet show for the neighborhood. Or best of all, he may just choose to hang out with mom or dad for a bit!

Somehow we must convince ourselves that time spent with our kids playing a game of monopoly, shooting hoops, or sharing a tea party reaps longer-lasting results than rushing from practice to practice and activity to activity. Kids are happier, more relaxed, more creative and less stressed when scheduled activities are limited. Their spirit soars!

Lets give our kids the gift of guidance in limiting their choices for organized activities. Our efforts won't give us medals or trophies to brag about, but our reward will be something far more valuable – their ability to make all decisions, including how they want to fill their leisure time.

In case I have piqued your interest, but not totally convinced you about the dangers of over-scheduling your child, I would like to recommend an excellent book. It is *The Over-Scheduled Child: Avoiding the Hyper-Parenting Trap* by Alvin Rosenfeld and Nicole Wise. The book was published in

April 2001. A review in the *New York Times* said, "This compelling, well-written book is a cautionary tale for parents who think that signing their children up for after school activities and lessons is always in their best interest." Of course I endorse this book because the authors' opinions coincide with mine (or maybe it's the other way around) on the topic of over-scheduling. If you're still "on the fence" about this issue, or need a bit more ammunition before you enact the policy in your home, read Rosenfeld and Wise's book. If I haven't convinced you that over-scheduling is detrimental to your child, they will. I promise!

If you're too busy to enjoy life, you're too busy.
                                                     -   Jeff Davidson

24

MARCHING TO A DIFFERENT DRUMMER

Few things tug at a parent's heart more forcefully than realizing her child doesn't "fit in." He marches to his own drummer in a one-man band, and mom tries to wipe away the tears. The child who doesn't fit the "regular kid" mold is often ignored, teased, or taunted. Any of these responses are painful to a child. A combination of two or three can (and often does) spell disaster. As was mentioned in Chapter 22, the long-range consequences for ostracized or perpetually teased kids are monumental.

Think back to what you have learned about the perpetrators of our country's horrific school-violence attacks. In almost every instance the shooters were loners, or kids that had been the butt of peer ridicule for most of their school career. I am not suggesting that every kid who is called a "stupid moron" or is never invited to a birthday party is going to ultimately bring a weapon to school or workplace and open fire. Far from it. But, make no mistake about it; negative ramifications do follow the left-out, teased kid all the way to adulthood. And those scars forever affect how he views himself and his fellowman. Therefore it is up to us as adults to do everything in our power to help these kids see themselves in a better light, aid them in sanding down their rough edges, and enhance their likelihood for peer acceptance.

There are four reasons that cause kids to be viewed as being "out of the loop." They include shyness, irritating behaviors, physical appearance, and personal choice. Before we look at these areas, I want to mention briefly the type of situation we are not talking about.

We are not referring to seven-year old Linda who reports to mom that her two best friends don't like her anymore. She "knows" this because they whispered to each other on the playground, and wouldn't share their secret with her. (She doesn't realize yet that when girls are involved, three is a crowd.) Nor are we talking about twelve-year-old Leslie who slams the phone down after hearing that her very best friend in the whole wide world has just invited "ugly-faced Kim" to a sleepover on Friday night. Disappointments like these are typical and normal (especially for females). Consider them for what they are - a rite of passage to womanhood. Although parents should not necessarily ignore (and certainly not ridicule) these complaints and frustrations, they need not lose a whole bunch of sleep over them. Disgruntlements like these are usually solved (without adult intervention) within forty-eight hours.

Now we'll discuss the kids we do need to be concerned about. These are the children (over the age of five) who never receive a phone call. They are never invited to a birthday party. They are always the last ones chosen for a team. They are constantly teased about some real or perceived imperfection. Many of these children are very unhappy, and most likely they view themselves as "losers."

First we'll look at the child who is excluded due to excessive shyness. This is the least common cause of rejection, the least serious, and the one that requires the least intervention.

The very shy child is rarely teased or taunted. He is much more likely to be "simply" ignored. Although this can be painful for the child, it is more likely to be painful to the parent. The shy child often takes comfort in being ignored because he isn't faced with the prospect of being around the gang, but not part of it. By contrast, the parent of the very shy child has the misguided expectation that his child will walk through life – forever alone. Realistically, this is simply not true. **Most shy children will eventually develop "normal" interaction skills without any drastic interventions**. There is however a few things parents can do to help speed up the maturational process that leads to better social interaction skills for the excessively shy child.

You can help your shy youngster by encouraging her to invite *one* kid to come for a "play-date" or a sleepover. Multi-kid parties for the very shy child are not recommended because they allow the shy one to be excluded (and feel very alone) while the others are tearing around having a raucous good time. This includes birthday parties.

Many well-intentioned parents have invited an entire classroom (or all the girls/boys) to a party honoring their shy child's birthday, only to see it backfire. Their little one hates the noise, the confusion, and the entire atmosphere. He would much prefer to entertain one friend for pizza, birthday cake, and a video. For the shy child, one gift is better than twenty. There aren't so many squabbles about who will get to play with which gift first!

Encourage (do not demand) your child's participation in *one* after-school activity or organization that you believe he will enjoy. Support his choice by showing interest in the groups' endeavors, and offering your assistance when possible. If your shy youngster is adamant about not joining a group, don't push it. Normally, the shy kid will sooner or later find another shy child to become friends with, and he will no longer be or feel totally alone. A kid does not need ten "best friends" in order to fit in. If he is comfortable having only one friend to hang out with, leave him alone.

Finally, give yourself a pep talk. Try to determine if it is your child that is unhappy with his aloneness, or if it is you that is distressed about his lack of popularity. Your evaluation of the situation will determine whether or not you need to attempt any kind of intervention. If your child is unhappy, get to work. If you are the only one concerned with the situation – relax. Remember, "Different folks respond to different strokes." Again, keep in mind the fact that time and maturity will most likely correct the situation.

Sometimes children are teased due to mannerisms or behaviors that cause other kids not to like them. This situation is much more difficult for parents to deal with because it means they must see their child as others see him, and then work to correct the situation.

The list of behaviors that turn other kids off can be pretty lengthy. A few that I observed in the classroom included bossiness, bragging, showing off, or loosing poorly. Constant touching, unwillingness to share, tattling, and whining were also common irritants. Even talking too often or laughing too loudly met with disapproval! Of course all kids occasionally resort to one or more of these behaviors, and it's no big deal. However, if one (or several) of these characteristics becomes a major part of the child's personality, there is a problem that needs to be addressed!

If you have observed (or been informed by the teacher) that your child exhibits one or more highly irritating behaviors, it is time to seek outside help. The chances are pretty high that he is being excluded, teased, or taunted both at school and in the neighborhood. HE NEEDS HELP, AND HE NEEDS IT NOW! It is vitally important that you not ignore irritating traits and mannerisms that you observe in your child. If they have been practiced for a period of time, they will not suddenly (or even eventually) magically disappear without some kind of intervention.

I suggest you start by contacting your child's teacher. Ask her to share her observations, and her perception of the problem. Ask if she has recommendations, and be prepared to follow through on any suggestions she might offer. If the teacher deems the problem as somewhat serious, she may want to solicit input and help from the school guidance counselor. If that is the case, embrace the idea. Three heads are better than two when it comes to problem solving.

If you conscientiously carry through on suggestions provided by the teacher and/or guidance counselor, you should see improvement within two to three months. If you do not, you may want to consult a certified child psychologist for further evaluation and help.

I want to repeat a caution that I mentioned in an earlier chapter because it is important that you expect it, prepare for it, and are not thrown for a loop when it happens. **Anytime you attempt to change a longstanding behavior, you may initially see a worsening of the behavior being targeted**. The kid is subconsciously hanging on for dear life to a behavior he is accustomed to, and he is making one last ditch effort not to let go. DO NOT GIVE UP! If you stick to your resolve, "that too shall pass." Eventually, your intervention efforts will help to make your child more acceptable to others, and he will be happier because of it.

Physical appearance is occasionally the cause for cruel and relentless teasing. Of course this does not occur in the classroom because NO teacher ever allows a child to be ridiculed in her presence. But kids find plenty of places and ways to inflict verbal abuse when they are out of an adult's earshot. And make no mistake about it – words do hurt – a lot!

Physical appearance presents a quandary because although some of it can be changed, much cannot.

You are all familiar with the famous Serenity prayer (written anonymously) that says: "God grant me the serenity to accept the things I cannot change – the courage to change the things I can – And the wisdom to know the difference." Let's look first at the things parents *can* change.

Parents can demand that their kids keep their bodies and hair clean, and free of odor. Poor hygiene is not a result of poverty. It is due to a lack of parental attention or training. And to put it quite bluntly – it is inexcusable! (Whew! That's one of the things I often wanted to say at parent-teacher conferences, but never dared to.)

Parents can provide their kids with appropriate clothing that fits properly and is free of rips and tears. Lack of money is an unacceptable excuse for a child coming to school looking like a refugee from a third-world country. A parent can utilize garage sales, family hand-me-downs, Goodwill, second-time-around stores, and Community Closets to help dress her child in an appropriate manner - a manner that will not prompt teasing and taunting.

If a child is being ridiculed about obesity, poor teeth, unusual walking gait, or a strange voice quality, the parent is wise to seek medical attention. If the suggested treatment is costly, physicians can provide information on agencies that offer financial assistance for those who qualify. Parents should not let pride prevent them from seeking financial help. This is their KID they are asking for, not themselves!

Realistically, some things about a child's appearance *cannot* be changed. The list is long, but the situation is far from hopeless. We cannot change things like freckles, physical disabilities, glasses, too tall, too short, too thin, too anything. So why aren't these situations hopeless? Because we can change how a child feels about his "imperfections" and about himself as a person.

Parents must instill in their child (and themselves) the realization that physical imperfections are only an outside covering. They have nothing whatsoever to do with what's inside.

An analogy I liked to use (every year) with my students was the "bedspread story." I would ask the kids to tell me about their bedspreads that they slept under each night. Each kid would describe his or her spread down to the very last detail, usually with a touch of pride. Then I asked them to pretend that mom suddenly discarded their beautiful spread and exchanged it with a yucky-colored, torn blanket of equal weight. How would they feel? Of course I heard "mad", "sad", and everything in between. When they were through expounding (or when I had heard enough and shut them off), I asked how their ugly bedspread changed them once they got under the covers – reminding them that it was as heavy (and therefore as warm) as their "beautiful" spread. Did their ugly spread cause them to lose their ability to laugh? Did it turn them into a mean and naughty kid? Did it prevent them from having fun with their friends the next day? Of course their responses ranged from "NO" to looks that said, "Have you lost your mind?" At that point I hit 'em with my sermon. It went like this.

"Our imperfections are nothing more than an ugly bedspread. They don't change or diminish what's underneath ONE LITTLE BIT." One "lecture" does not miraculously transform a child suffering from feelings of inferiority into one who is full of confidence and self-assurance, but that type of mindset (if repeated often enough and by enough caring adults) will get the job done.

Demonstrate through your words and actions - every single day - that you believe your child has many qualities that cause him to be lovable and worthy of respect. The list of wonderful, unique attributes that help make a person likeable and special (and have nothing to do with physical characteristics) is endless. A beautiful smile, a caring attitude, good manners, and a sense of humor are things that have always endeared me to a child. I bet your list is much longer when you contemplate your youngster. Never miss an opportunity to tell and show your child that you love him because of his special and unique assets, not because of what is or is not on the outside "cover."

Use opportunities to draw attention to the popular, successful celebrity who is not blessed with an appealing physical appearance. Every walk of life is filled with individuals who fit this description – including teachers. Use their success as an example, an inspiration, and an incentive. When you hear of or see an individual who has overcome huge physical limitations and gone on to succeed or excel in a particular endeavor, discuss it with your child. To summarize, remind your youngster on a regular basis (in one way or another) that YOU CAN'T JUDGE A BOOK BY ITS COVER!

I have one final suggestion for the parent of a teased child. Tell your youngster (or remind him) that the person doing the teasing is the one who has the problem. The child (or adult) who ridicules others does not feel very good about himself, so he attempts to feel better by putting someone else down. The teased child needs to be told this fact – repeatedly - until he internalizes it. When a teased child understands that the problem is not with him, but with the perpetrator, harmful effects are drastically minimized.

At this point I want to answer a question you may be wondering about. Why didn't I mention the seriously mentally or physically handicapped child when I spoke of conditions that are beyond our power to change? The reason is really quite simple. **During my forty-two years of teaching, I never once saw a child tease or taunt a <u>profoundly</u> handicapped child.** (Even bullies have some sense of common decency!) I chose not to address the issue because I don't believe it is a problem.

On rare occasions, a child is excluded from group activity by his own choice. Although some experts say this is never the case, I believe that it is! Why do I make such a bold statement? Because I've seen it happen. Occasionally a child is completely comfortable with himself; he enjoys playing alone and doesn't feel the need to be a part of a group. This one characteristic (if not accompanied by other red flags) does not signify autism. It simply means the child is unique and enjoys his solitude.

If your child is contented with his aloneness, let him be. It doesn't mean he will enter adulthood as a hermit, or is destined to assume the role of a billionaire computer geek unable to relate to people! (Of course the billionaire part of that equation doesn't sound too bad.) It simply means that at this stage in his life, he prefers to travel solo. If your child doesn't complain about mistreatment from others, and appears happy marching to his own drummer, let him be. It may not be the kind of beat you march to, or the kind his teacher marches to, but that doesn't necessarily make it wrong.

In this chapter we discussed things that you can do to help the teased or excluded child. There are also a few things to avoid.

- Do *not* heap on sympathy for every minor emotional hurt your child suffers. If you do, he'll feel that he has been terribly mistreated and that justice needs to be served. Listen – always. React – seldom.

- Do *not* get involved by calling another child's mother when your child has been omitted from a party invitation. It's sure to backfire. Assist your child in planning a pleasurable alternative activity for the party timeslot.

- Do not project your own desire for popularity on to your child. Maybe your daughter doesn't *want* to be Homecoming Queen, and freeze her "tush" in the parade. Perhaps your son doesn't *want* the responsibilities that go along with being a football captain! Allow them the freedom to do what feels comfortable to them, not you.

We are each gifted in a unique and important way. It is our privilege to discover our own special light.

- Mary Dunbar

25

NO MAGIC NUMBER

At the same time I made the painful decision to retire, I decided not to do any substitute teaching - except in cases of dire emergency. My love for teaching was largely due to the satisfaction I felt as I watched "my" kids grow in confidence and develop their skills. I did not think substituting would offer that same joy.

Most children entered my first grade classroom knowing the names of the alphabet letters and some of their sounds. When they left they were reading chapter books! They came in recognizing numerals to five. They left with a firm grip on addition, subtraction, counting money, and telling time. Most children knew how to write their first name when they came into my room. By the end of first grade, they were able to write a hundred-word short story. For me (and I suspect most teachers), their academic, emotional, and maturational growth was a magical process to watch. I knew substituting would not allow me to see that growth. It would be primarily (in my mind, at least) a "babysitting" job, and I never was overly fond of babysitting – until my grandkids appeared on the scene. In addition to that, substitute teachers are paid less than babysitters!

With a few exceptions, I stuck to my resolve and turned down numerous requests to substitute. I was writing this book. I was doing some volunteer work. I was mentoring in a former colleague's classroom, and I was getting to spend more time with my grandchildren. I did not need to substitute in order to fill my time. And then – in early April – I received one of those "emergency" calls.

A substitute was needed for a kindergarten room in the nearby community of Rowley, Iowa (population 290). The Kindergarten through 5th building where I was asked to sub (officially named South Elementary) was a satellite attendance center for the semi-large district where I had concluded my teaching career. South Elementary had very small classes and a strong commitment of support from their community. They also enjoyed (and had earned) a reputation for excellence. And, like hundreds of other small schools across the country, they were embroiled in a heated battle to keep their small school open.

Donalyn Pogue was the regular teacher in the room where I was asked to sub. Donalyn and I had taught together in earlier years, and I knew she was a master teacher. Her kids would be well trained. But...they were kindergarteners, and I had strong reservations. I had a distinct recollection of subbing the prior September in a different kindergarten room. Memories of that day kept flashing through my mind as I recalled 19 little live wires who had short attention spans and loud voices. I remembered the 19 bundles of energy that didn't care who they talked to, or if anyone listened. I smiled to myself as I recalled how 19 kids had jumped, skipped, hopped, and ran to the various learning centers, stayed two minutes – and then moved on.

But, subs are hard to come by in April and May. Teachers that have not already used their allotted day for personal-leave are intent on "using it instead of losing it." Therefore, with some reluctance (and a sense of loyalty to my profession), I agreed to fill in for Mrs. Pogue.

Well, I was in for a shock. Those kindergarteners (eleven in the class) were absolutely amazing. They were polite. They knew all the rules, and they followed them. They read far above and beyond what is normally expected of kindergarteners in early April. They were even quiet during their "rest and read" time. Wow! I was – putting it mildly – impressed.

At the end of my delightful day at South, I felt compelled to contact Mrs. Pogue and congratulate her on a JOB WELL DONE. She thanked me for the compliment, but refused to accept any credit. She said, "I really am not doing anything differently than I always have. I think their extraordinary success is due to the fact that it is an unusually small class, and they are a bunch of little go-getters. They literally soak up everything I present, and beg for more. It's one of those classes you dream about, but rarely see."

Although I think Mrs. Pogue was being a bit too humble in her refusal to accept credit, she certainly made a valid point. The size of a class and the *makeup of its members* do have a direct correlation to student achievement.

Am I going to suggest that schools limit their classrooms to eleven kids? No, I certainly am not. Although that would be nice, it most definitely would be unrealistic. The national average size for a kindergarten class is 26 students. That is double the size of South Elementary, plus four. No, we can't afford to have classes with eleven kids, but neither can kids afford to have their teacher's time and attention divided by 26. We must find the "happy" medium, and then unearth a way to pay for it.

In 1999, five States — IOWA, MARYLAND, MINNESOTA, NEW YORK, and WISCONSIN — enacted new initiatives or significantly expanded existing initiatives to lower class size. As of this writing, 20 States have class size reduction initiatives in place. Their plans are not "freebies" where the state government doles out money, tells schools to have fun, and then rides off into the sunset. No way! The grants come with heavy price tags of paperwork, forms, assessment, and reporting. If procedures aren't followed, or if standardized test scores fail to rise – POOF! The money stops. The plans (all similar, but with variations) are not perfect, but they certainly help.

Most lower-elementary rooms in these twenty states now have a cap of twenty students per classroom. These small primary level classes are extremely valuable in getting five-year-olds off to a good start, and they should be mandatory throughout our country. If our politicians really want "to leave no child behind", they will enact this policy at the federal level, and supply the necessary funding. A few brave elected officials have introduced legislation designed for this purpose, but they have been unsuccessful in getting it passed into law.

On February 15, 2001, Missouri Senator Jean Carnahan (D) introduced her first piece of legislation, The *Quality Classrooms Act,* to the Senate. The *Quality Classrooms Act* was based on a proposal made by Carnahan's late husband, Missouri Governor Mel Carnahan, during his campaign for the Senate seat. The bill was designed to help local school districts reduce class size and improve classroom instruction. It called for **$50 billion** (not exactly pocket change) to be distributed to local school districts over a period of ten years. The funds were to have gone directly from the federal government to local school districts - bypassing much of the existing bureaucracy. Eighty percent of the funds were to be allocated on the proportion of children in a district living in poverty, and twenty percent on the district's relative enrollment.

The *Quality Classrooms Act* recognized that different districts have different needs. Instead of mandating a one-size-fits-all approach, it included a "Local Accountability Menu."

The plan gave local school districts the flexibility of choosing one of (or a combination of) five options to help address their local classroom needs.

A small portion of Senator Carnahan's proposal was incorporated into a "sweeping education reform plan" that was agreed to by the White House and congress, but ultimately defeated. Apparently the politicians who (prior to the election of 2000) were going to "make education their number one priority", had a lapse of memory or a change of heart. Or maybe they were just too busy working on their mantra for the 2002 election - a promise "to spend all their energies on legislation designed to lower the price of prescription drugs." I can't help but wonder about what happened to the commitment they made to education only two short years earlier. Perhaps it got lost somewhere in the pile of Florida ballots.

Because very small children need the most individual attention, they need the smallest classes. Kindergarten, first and second grade is where the foundation for learning is laid. It is also where children form their attitudes about learning. Small primary grade classes help to ensure that kids will get the kind of start that they need. Good skills and positive attitudes learned in the early grades enable students to continue their education in slightly larger classes as they progress to the intermediate grades and beyond.

There is no "magic" class size that is affordable for every district, and there is no magic number of students that will guarantee success. However, statistical research suggests a maximum number of 20 at the primary level as a reasonable goal to target. Research also indicates that fourth grades and above can usually function adequately with 25 students. (My teaching experience leads me to believe that these higher numbers usually do allow maximum learning to take place.)

However, sometimes the numbers need to be adjusted due to the composition of a particular group of students.

Occasionally a majority of the kids in a class present traits so similar that the class takes on a distinct "flavor" of its own. (By class, I mean the grade – not a section. Example: a school might have six sections in their second grade class.) I do not understand (and therefore cannot explain) how a class takes on personality of its own, but I know it happens - frequently. When this situation occurs, a class is often referred to (discreetly, I hope) as Jocks, Brains, Hell-raisers, Preppies, Numbskulls, or some other "descriptive" label. Of course there are always students who do not fit the label, but they are surrounded and affected by those who do. Strangely, when this phenomenon occurs it is often observable from kindergarten all the way through twelfth grade.

Although "flavorful" classes do not always present special challenges, they quite often do. If a class has an abnormally high number of students with low ability, delayed achievement, or serious disruptive behaviors, it should be divided into smaller than average sections. If we apply numbers to such a recommendation, it might look like this. One hundred "average" fifth graders could be placed into four sections, whereas a "challenging" group of 100 fifth graders would be better served in five sections.

Frequently (more often than not) the number of children enrolled in a particular grade doesn't exactly fit within the maximum limit, but the "overflow" isn't enough to warrant adding a section. That is when the composition of the grade should be the determining factor.

For example, 109 average third graders should be able to succeed adequately when divided into four sections. If that situation occurs, teachers should bite the bullet and their tongues – and hope for a smaller class the following year. By contrast, an extremely challenging or particularly needy group of 109 third graders should to be divided into five sections. Only then will it be possible for them to receive adequate attention and experience maximum learning opportunities. (Such a plan also helps the teacher maintain her sanity.)

When school boards make their annual decisions about class size, they should listen to the principal's assessment of the general makeup for each grade, and then act accordingly. They need to remember that there is no such thing as, "one size fits all" when it comes to class size. There is no magic number to fit every situation. Predetermined guidelines are fine, but there will always be exceptions. When those exceptions arise, decisions need to be made not on cost or ease of implementation, but on what is best for kids.

A recommendation like the one I am suggesting is not easy for anyone. In some cases, school board members will be faced with the daunting task of finding enough money to hire an additional teacher. Taxpayers will be forced to dig even deeper into their already stretched pockets. Principals will be given the miserable job of informing teachers that their teaching assignments or their classrooms will be changed in order to compensate for the needs of a "special" group. And one or more teachers will be assigned to teach a grade different from what he has become accustomed to, and has gathered materials for. But, everyone involved must put his personal preferences aside, cope with the inconveniences, and focus on the school's mission of educating students.

Yes, making exceptions for a particularly needy group of kids is tough, but we want *all* kids to have the best possible opportunity for success. If that requires some belt tightening and sacrificing, so be it. If called upon, we need to "seize the moment", and do what's right for kids. They are our future, and we need to invest in them wisely.

In a moment of decision, the best thing you can do is the right thing to do. The worst thing you can do is nothing.
-Theodore Roosevelt

26

FORGET THE LAWYER

In February, 2001, the news media related the story of Christine Pelton, a biology teacher in the rural school district of Piper, Kansas. Reportedly, Ms. Pelton accused several students of cheating through plagiarism (copying word for word) from the Internet while completing a science project on tree leaves. At that point she received her district's backing. When the same offense happened a second time, Ms. Pelton failed the 28 sophomores whom she discovered had once again plagiarized material from the Internet. Her principal and superintendent agreed. It was plagiarism and the students should get a zero for the assignment. But, parents complained and the Piper School Board ordered Ms. Pelton to go easier on the guilty students. Ms. Pelton resigned her teaching position in protest. (Ms. Pelton left the teaching profession and has not returned.)

The next story also occurred in the Midwest. In March of 1999, the Linn-Mar High School band of Marion, Iowa took a chaperoned bus trip to Texas for the purpose of performing. Band director Steve Colton found student Tony Ette with a pack of cigarettes after a chaperone reported smelling cigarette smoke coming from Tony's San Antonio hotel room. Smoking cigarettes was against the rules set down before the school sponsored trip and was clearly spelled out in the district's co-curricular handbook. Band director Colton talked with Tony, then 15, at which time he admitted that he had smoked en route to San Antonio (in the *bus*), but denied smoking in his hotel room. He showed no remorse and refused to agree to discontinue smoking for the remainder of the trip.

After considerable contemplation, Mr. Colton made the decision to send Tony home - alone - on a bus. Colton stood by Tony's side as the boy called his father and told him that he was being sent home on a bus, and the reason for it. Several hours later, instructor Colton accompanied Tony to the bus depot for the 11:55 p.m. bus departure, and once again stood by Tony's side as the boy called his father to provide him with the details of the 30-hour trip.

When band director Colton returned to Marion with his students, he was advised that he, along with the associate director of bands, and the Superintendent of schools were being sued by Tony's father for putting Tony on a bus without a chaperone. The civil lawsuit was heard in Linn County District Court where the case was dismissed by a ruling that stated schools, like other governmental entities, are exempt from being sued for its decisions, whether right or wrong. In December 2002, the Iowa Supreme Court overturned that decision, and as of this writing (September, 2003), the case is still pending.

The common thread between the two stories I just shared is that in both cases, the parents did not want their kids held accountable for their actions. In essence, they were saying their children should not have been made to face the consequences of their misbehavior.

I believe that both of these accounts might cause us to examine some uncomfortable questions. Questions such as: When do I support my kid? When do I defend my child? When should I enable my youngster to continue to make poor choices? And finally, when should I stand back and allow my kid to suffer the consequences of his actions?

Let's start with the easiest question first. When should I support my kid if he has "blown it" and committed a minor offense or even an egregious act? The answer is, ALWAYS! Support means to assist, to help, to lean on. As parents, we are mandated to do this in the bad times as well as in the good times. It is important we understand and internalize the fact that supporting is not necessarily synonymous with condoning.

When we condone an action, we are indicating we feel the misbehavior is no big deal and does not deserve punishment. Condoning is accomplished through a variety of methods. It might be with words of concealment or denial. It might be through a threat or an act of intimidation. And at the extreme level, it is the initiation of a lawsuit intended to harm (or destroy) the person or group responsible for prescribing the child's punishment. All of these responses send an unstated message to the child that says, "Go ahead and screw up. I'll protect you, no matter what!"

Supporting a child means that we will stand with him as he faces the consequences of his actions. We will not send him to live with Grandma and then move without leaving a forwarding address. Neither will we allow Big Sister to refer to him as "the loser." We'll offer our love and encouragement. We'll walk beside him as he "faces his music." We'll let him know that we have faith in him as a worthy human being, and that we firmly expect he will learn from this experience and it's consequences, and that he will not repeat the same offense again. (We don't need to let him see the fingers we have crossed behind our back!) In short, we'll let him know that we will always love him, but we will *never* condone flagrant misbehavior!

The issue of defending our kids is a bit murkier. We need to defend our kids when we have listened to all sides of the issue (or offense) and have determined that our child has indeed been unfairly accused or is about to be unjustly punished for something he didn't do. When that situation occurs, we are obligated to defend him. To do less would be abdicating our responsibility as a parent. However, a word of caution is in order.

It is extremely natural for a parent to look through rose-colored glasses when viewing a situation that involves an accusation regarding his offspring. A parent not only wants to see his child in a favorable light, but he wants others to view him in that same glow. In many cases a parent simply cannot decide exactly where the truth lies, and what the best course of action is.

When that situation occurs (and at some time or other it WILL,) it is perhaps wise to solicit an opinion from a neutral third party. Sorry, but grandparents and best friends are not good choices. Grandparents always think their grandkids are perfect (I *know* mine are), and a best friend doesn't want to say something that will hurt or offend his pal. A wiser pool of candidates might include a religious leader, a respected co-worker, or an uninvolved teacher. The "go-between" can usually render an unbiased opinion because he doesn't have the same emotional involvement as does the parent and the teacher.

If after going through these steps you still believe your child was falsely accused or treated unfairly, then by all means – DEFEND him! If your final assessment of the situation suggests your child was in the wrong, then SUPPORT him as he faces the consequences of his actions.

When do we enable a kid by concealing information or covering up for him, and thereby allow him to continue making poor choices? The answer to this one is simple – NEVER!

Let's pretend your teenage daughter wants to go to the mall to buy a new gown for the upcoming formal. You call the school to say she is "sick" and unable to be in school that day. You are enabling her to be miss class, and you are also being untruthful. (That's not a winning combination!) Or, let's pretend your high school athlete is banned from competition due to an accusation of consuming alcohol at a weekend party, which in fact he did do You dust off Grandma's bible and swear that he was home with you all weekend playing board games. He couldn't possibly have been at that party. Again, you are enabling him to engage in untruthfulness for the purpose of avoiding punishment. I can think of no time when it is even remotely productive to enable a child to continue actions that might lead to self-destructive, adult behavior. Not ever!

At this point we need to look at the really tough question – the Granddaddy of them all. **When do I allow my kid to suffer the consequences of his poor choices**? For starters, you must develop a case of far-sightedness. Try looking into the future and decide whether or not you want your child to continue the same type of behavior that has gotten him into trouble at this point in time. If you honestly do not want his poor choices accompanying him to adulthood, then you need to allow him to suffer the consequences for his actions *now*. Now is when his values are being shaped. And now is when you are there to support him, help him pick up the pieces, and guide him as he moves on toward becoming a happy, productive, contributing adult.

Will your child come rushing at you, throw his arms around you, and thank you for making him suffer the consequences of his actions? Heavens to Betsy, no! (At least not for another fifteen years or so.) But try to remember this. What kids may view as intolerance, heavy-handedness, insensitivity, and coercion on your part, is really MASTER PARENTING.

Is this easy? Absolutely not! We all want to protect our kids from pain and discomfort. When they are hurting, we feel as though someone knocked the wind out of us. When they are humiliated, we cry for them and with them. When they are disciplined for a poor choice, our heart aches for them. But such is the cost of parenting. It comes with a huge price tag, but the finished product is worth the investment.

To become emotionally mature, children must learn from failure and face the consequences of their poor choices. As parents, we must develop the courage to let it happen. We need to allow them to suffer the pain of the present in order to pay for the joy and fulfillment of the future.

Failure is nothing to celebrate, but it can be a potent teacher.

- Abigale Van Buren

27

SHOULD WE OR SHOULDN'T WE?

Most people recognize the value of a cooperative and friendly parent-teacher relationship. They understand that the effort of one without the cooperation of the other is an exercise in futility. During my teaching tenure I was fortunate to work with hundreds of wonderful, caring parents who tried their very hardest to do what they considered to be in the best interests of their children. I doubt that my experience was unique to that of countless other teachers across the country.

Unfortunately, there was one situation in my teaching career that invariably tested this bond of cooperation. It involved retention. Over a period of forty-two years, I felt compelled to recommend retention on eight different occasions. It was seldom pleasant, and it was never easy.

The "I-hate-to-tell-you-this-but..." meeting normally took place in early spring. My recommendation was usually received with an amount of enthusiasm equal to that of finding a rotten egg in the Easter basket. Although it wasn't always verbalized, most parents thought the idea stunk!

The speech (always delivered after a sleepless night) went something like this. "I want you to know how much I care for "Teddy." He is a bright little guy, and a true joy to have in the classroom. However, after thinking the matter over carefully and considering all the options, I would like to recommend that we retain Teddy in first grade."

Boom. The parents' life, as they had known it five minutes earlier, suddenly came to a screeching halt. They were momentarily convinced that life would never again hold the same joy and satisfaction that it had before Teacher dropped the bombshell.

Yes, they knew that school for Teddy was not a case of peaches dripping with cream. They had attended all of the regularly scheduled conferences, and had been informed that there were deficiencies. But they had tried so hard!

They had looked at Teddy's school papers in the evening. They had attempted (often unsuccessfully) to entice him to sit down and work on the areas that were causing him difficulty. They had made a special private study area for him where he could work undisturbed. (Unfortunately, the study area also housed a computer that was simply great for playing games.) They had cried, screamed, and bribed. They had taken away privileges and promised rewards. They had purchased an expensive tutorial. And now the teacher was telling them that the problem was still not solved. They wondered how this could have happened to them and to *their* child. They wondered what they had done wrong.

For those of you who have not had a child with academic difficulties, you may be surprised to learn that most parents of failing students have done nothing wrong. A student's failure to master a required amount of material within a specified timeframe simply means that something hasn't worked right for that particular child. It is a situation that always requires cooperative problem solving. It is also a situation that occasionally calls for retention. Blame should be not be assigned to the child, the parent, or the teacher when retention is suggested. Blaming (of one's self or others) serves no purpose, and it solves no problems.

This chapter is written for the parents who may someday face the issue of retention. It is also for all interested people who want to understand when retention is appropriate, and when it is not. I hope this chapter will...

- Help all readers understand how *some* low achievers are best served by social promotion, whereas others might benefit from retention.

- Empower parents with the resolve to stop beating themselves up emotionally if retention is recommended.

- Encourage parents to understand that retention should be viewed as an opportunity for the future rather than as a failure of the past.

- Provide parents with concrete ideas that will help them decide whether or not retention would be beneficial for their child.

There are few areas in education where we speak out of both corners of our mouths as often as we do in matters that relate to retention. It is common to hear an individual vehemently denounce the popular current practice of "social promotion" (promoting a student to the next grade level without having successfully completed the requirements of his current grade) until he himself faces the dilemma. When retention is suggested for *his* child, his position changes quickly and dramatically. He says (by innuendo), "You should insist that your kid be "flunked" if he can't cut the mustard, but I'm not going to allow it to happen it to mine!" (Incidentally, I consider the word "flunked" as offensive as any other "f" word you might think of.)

Two decades ago, retention was an accepted practice for students who had not successfully completed all grade or subject requirements within a school year. And then statisticians entered the scene. Between 1980 and 1985, dozens of studies were conducted that indicated retention was rarely beneficial, and often harmful. During that same timeframe, parents were given the opportunity to make the final decision (formally reserved for the teacher and principal) regarding retention. The end result was an almost total elimination of retention.

In the late 1990's statisticians again went into action, and several new studies were conducted. The latter studies found that **retention does have merit for the struggling or failing student IF the child possesses average or above average ability.** (My classroom experience with more than 1500 students causes me to accept and embrace the conclusions of these most recent studies.)

"All men are created equal." This quote comes of course from the Declaration of Independence, and as far as human worth and value - it is irrefutable. If, however, we think of it as meaning that all kids are "created with equal capabilities and opportunities," we are being unrealistic.

The number of differing abilities in every classroom is always equal to the number of students enrolled in that room. Although most of us are aware of and understand this wide ability range, we still continue to expect all kids to learn the same amount of material within a specified timeframe. Is this realistic? No. Is it possible? No, again.

I believe that we need to make retention decisions on the basis of the student's perceived mental capacity. **The child who has limited or very low intellect is rarely** (if ever) **going to profit from retention**. An additional year of covering the same material with a low-ability student does nothing more than to reinforce an already low self-concept and increase feelings of hostility and worthlessness.

Throughout our country more than a few kids have completed thirteen years of school and are still unable to read and comprehend beyond a third grade level. Would their reading prowess or overall achievement improved significantly had they been retained in third grade for ten years? Hardly!

One thing, however, is certain. If we choose (or are forced) to follow the demands of policy makers who insist a student not be promoted until all academic requirements of a grade or subject are met, the results will be disastrous. (Remember: The No Child Left Behind legislation demands that every kid test at a proficient level in reading, math, and science.) Trust me, the self-concepts of extremely low achievers will be poorer than the D's and F's on their progress reports if we abide by the "proficient or else" ultimatum. Behaviors will be intolerable. The student's adult life will most likely revolve around poverty, jail, prison, a mental health facility, or (due to suicide, drug or alcohol abuse) the mortuary. These results are unacceptable. They are also avoidable.

Some children are mentally incapable of grasping a full year's curriculum in nine months - no matter how hard they try or how good the teacher is! These kids don't need the "punishment" of retention. They need the "reward" of support as they continue their struggle to achieve to the best of their ability. Adults should choose their words to match what they know in their hearts to be true. They would also be wise to look over the music before they hop on the bandwagon that demands an end to *all* social promotion.

In contrast to the low ability student, some children possess average ability or above, but achieve at a lower level than their peers. In other words, they fail to complete grade or subject requirements in the allotted timeframe despite having an adequate amount of "gray matter." A few of the factors that contribute to this situation include young age, delayed maturation, health problems, lack of emotional support, changing family makeup, or frequent transfers to different schools. These are the students that can profit from a "catch up" year, especially if the situation or condition that initially caused them to fall behind has been rectified – or at least improved.

In today's schools, only a miniscule number of children are retained because most parents refuse to grant permission. One might wonder why parental permission is required to enforce retention. Shouldn't the teacher's recommendation be enough to insure compliance? Yes... and no.

Past experience has demonstrated clear and convincing evidence that indicates retention is beneficial *only* when it is accompanied by unconditional parental support. Children are masters at detecting parental disappointment, disillusionment, and anger – typical reactions to a retention recommendation. It makes no difference whether the negative feelings are directed at the child, the teacher, the principal, or all of the above. The message the child hears is one that says, "YOU HAVE FAILED." In his eyes, he is a loser. His parents are upset, and he must be at fault. Unfortunately, the failing (or under-achieving) child's perception of guilt breeds further academic and emotional problems. The bottom line is this: **A retained student's future success is doomed, if retention is not entered into with unconditional parental support.**

Why are most parents adamantly opposed to retaining their child? The verbalized rationalizations are endless. Common ones include, "Her friends will tease her" and, "He does it at home, so we know he can do it. We'll work with him over the summer." I have often suspected that the real reason many parents view retention negatively is because they somehow feel it is a reflection on their ability to produce and rear a "smart" kid. That perception is as common as it is false.

What happens when a parent refuses to grant permission to retain his average or above-average ability child who is failing academically? A mentally capable youngster loses the opportunity to become an academic leader instead of one that forever is at the back-end of the learning line, gazing longingly toward the front.

Parents who receive a recommendation to retain their child need consider only two questions. 1."Does my child have the mental ability to realistically expect success if given another opportunity at the same grade level?" 2."Will another year of age (maturity) make success more probable for my child?" Reasons such as, "What will Grandma say?" or "I don't want my (neighbors, friends, co-workers) to find out," have no merit whatsoever when retention is being considered.

All parents experience extreme difficulty in being totally open-minded when it comes to making decisions that involve painful, difficult issues concerning their children. This reaction is both universal and understandable. It happens (repeatedly) because parents love their kids, and are so attached emotionally that they cannot see the forest for the trees.

If a parent finds herself in the dilemma of making a decision regarding retention, I strongly advise her to rely on the teacher's observations and recommendation. Although teachers love their students, that love is far different from what a parent feels. Furthermore, the teacher has the advantage of seeing the child in comparison to his peers of a similar age and grade level. In short, she has the insight and the lack of bias that a parent cannot possibly have. A parent is wise to listen to the teacher, to trust her professional judgment, and to thank her for recommending what she believes to be the wisest course of action. When all is said and done, it's better to look back and say "At least I tried," than to look back and say, "If only..."

You always pass failure on your way to success.
                                                              - Mickey Rooney

28

KEY TO SUCCESS

I have a multiple-choice question for you. You may pick only one answer, and NO FAIR PEEKING at the answer!

Q: **What has the greatest effect on your child's success in school?**

       a. Child's intelligence

       b. Money spent on education

       c. Parental involvement

       d. Quality of teachers

The answer is C.

You might doubt this answer, or you might even vehemently disagree with it. However, *I* believe it to be true, and recent studies concur. This is what Bruce and Christine Baron and Bonnie MacDonald say in *What Did You Learn in School Today?* "In the last 15 years, every major study on this topic has concluded that parents' involvement has more

219

influence on children's success in school than the quality of the teachers or the school."

In 1986 the US Department of Education published a study called *"What Works – Research about Teaching and Learning."* An excerpt from the study states, "Parents are their children's first and most influential teachers. What parents do to help their children learn is more important to academic success than how well-off the family is." The passage of time has not changed that assessment.

The awesome responsibility of active, positive parental involvement can provoke a variety of negative emotions. A parent might experience anger and respond with, "I already have a job. Teaching my child is the school's responsibility." Or, "I contribute an enormous amount of tax money to pay for teachers. Why should I be expected to do their job?" A parent might experience feelings of frustration as he contemplates his already full plate of responsibilities and wonders how it is possible to find time to be involved in his child's education. Perhaps he has feelings of helplessness because he doesn't know what to do or how to do it. And finally, he may suffer pangs of guilt as he ultimately decides he does not have the time, the energy or the ability to become actively involved in his child's learning.

All of the above emotions are understandable, and especially so if the child is struggling in school. The parent may have already spent a LOT of time with his child in an attempt to enhance his academic pursuits. He has probably nagged him to do his homework, or even done it for him. (Shame, shame.) He has perhaps pressured him to get better grades, threatened him with restrictions, or even punished him for his lack of effort. And ultimately, many have had to face the fact that all their efforts have produced no permanent improvements.

If you are a parent and this scenario sounds familiar, you're most likely looking for help. Well, that's why I have written this book. Drop that towel you're tempted to throw in, and grab your "I can do this" cloth. I want to share five suggestions that I believe will help. I am thoroughly confident that these ideas will enable all of you to provide the kind of positive parental participation that will increase the likelihood of your child's academic success.

I first encountered variations of these methods in the book *Positive Involvement* by Jack and Marsha Youngblood. They made sense to me, and I hope they do to you also.

- **Have realistic goals**

- **Expect success**

- **Recognize efforts**

- **Minimize reaction to failures**

- **Celebrate progress**

We'll briefly examine each suggestion.

Have realistic goals. It is extremely important that you understand what your child is capable of and expect his work to be consistent with his capabilities. To expect more than he is capable of invites failure and borders on cruelty. To expect less than he is capable of fosters mediocrity and is an injustice to your child.

If you are unsure of your child's ability and/or potential, discuss it with the teacher. The teacher is in a position to see your child on a daily basis in the academic setting. He has the opportunity to observe and to compare your child's achievement with that of other children in his age group. He also has the benefit of experience, and the luxury of less emotional involvement.

If "making a better grade" is a goal, experts suggest you strive for one increment at a time. A kid can see that raising a grade from a D to a C is attainable and worth the effort. Any expectation of raising a D to an A within one grading period is unrealistic and almost doomed to failure. When a student believes a goal is impossible to achieve, he won't exert much (or any) effort. He suspects that eventually you will give up and shut up! He decides (perhaps subconsciously) that he can outwait you. So be content with "baby" steps. It will take longer to reach the destination, but the reward is worth the trip.

Expect success. In almost every teacher's conference or symposium I attended throughout my teaching career I listened to the speaker say something similar to this. "Kids will fulfill your expectations. If you expect them to misbehave on the field trip, they will. If you expect them to do well on Friday's spelling test, they will." I'll be the first to admit that when I heard this speech during my early years of teaching, I thought it was a bunch of malarkey. Now, with more than four decades of teaching behind me, I know it to be true.

Tell your child what you expect in regard to his academic performance (remember, be realistic) or behavior, and more often than not he will meet your expectations. Caution: Kids are geniuses at interpreting emotions that differ from the spoken word. It does no good whatsoever to tell your child you expect him to complete his homework each evening, if your tone and demeanor suggest you're wasting your voice on a hopeless cause.

Recognize effort. Attempt to put your focus on your child's effort rather than on an achieved or desired grade such as A, B, or C. Did she finish her homework at a reasonable hour last evening? Did she turn in her homework? Did she arrive at class with the materials that she was expected to have? Did she complete the work she was expected to do at school that day? (Initially, and thereafter on a sporadic basis, you may need to verify your child's responses with the teacher.)

When improved effort becomes a habit, positive results will follow. These results include greater confidence, higher self-esteem, increased skill for learning, and finally – better grades.

Minimize reaction to failures. Authors Jack and Marsha Youngblood advise parents to ignore failures. I think that is going a bit too far. I suggest you minimize your reaction to failures, and focus on the effort that is necessary to achieve improvement. It does little or no good to nag, scream, ground, or take away privileges in reaction to a failure. Neither is anything positive gained by dictating ultimatums, threatening or bribing. That energy can be better used to develop with your student, a plan for improvement.

Your chances for success are considerably greater when you allow your child to have input in the plan of action and enable him to feel that he is working to meet his goals. (Of course, they're really your goals, but you don't need to broadcast that!) In other words, give him "ownership" of the plan, and he'll work his tail off to accomplish it.

Celebrate progress. All human beings react positively to praise. When the boss acknowledges your good work, what do you do? You work even harder because praise feels mighty good! When hubby compliments you on the great spaghetti and meatballs you cooked for dinner, what do you do? You give him spaghetti and meatballs the next four nights in a row! (Well, that might be a bit of an exaggeration, but you get the point.)

Kids react positively when praise follows positive effort and earned progress. (They are not fooled by feigned praise if it follows a poor effort.) Never let an opportunity slip by when you can celebrate or acknowledge improvement – no matter how small. The dividends far outweigh the investment.

There are many rewards for positive parental involvement, and they are all mighty gratifying. Your child's confidence will increase. He will show a more positive attitude. His behavior will improve at home and in school. He will earn higher grades. He will score higher on standardized tests. Ultimately, he will be happier, and so will you!

What God is to the world, parents are to their children.
-Philo

29

THE REAL SCOOP

A book from the Teacher's Desk would be incomplete without taking an "up close and personal look" at the men and women throughout our country who protect, direct, guide, teach, and love our kids.

We expect a lot from our teachers. We expect them to fill our kids' minds with a love for learning. We believe they should instill a sense of pride in each student's ethnicity, modify disruptive behavior, and watch for signs of emotional, physical, and sexual abuse. We want them to fight the war on drugs and sexually transmitted diseases, check students' backpacks for guns, and raise their self-esteem.

They are to teach patriotism, good citizenship, sportsmanship, and fair play. We expect our teachers to show kids how and where to vote, how to balance a checkbook, and how to apply for a job. They are to check heads occasionally for lice, maintain a safe environment, recognize signs of potential antisocial behavior, and offer advice. We want them to willingly write letters of recommendation for student employment and scholarships, and encourage respect for the cultural diversity and sexual preference of others.

We require them (by contract) to continually work toward advanced certification, attend after-school faculty meetings, serve on committees, participate in staff development training, and attend an "appropriate number" of conferences that relate to the subject matter they teach. And this is to be done on their personal time (summers and evenings) and at their own expense.

Teachers are mandated to serve as class sponsors, and assist at school-sponsored musical, athletic, and drama events. They are expected to demonstrate "appropriate interest" in all student endeavors. They are required to collect data, maintain records to support and document student progress, and then forward the information to the appropriate state and federal governmental offices. Teachers are directed to incorporate technology in their teaching, and simultaneously monitor all web sites for appropriateness. And of course, this is to be done while they provide a personal one-on-one relationship with each student.

Teachers can be held criminally liable if they fail to report suspicions about a student who might be potentially dangerous, or suffering some form of harassment and/or abuse. And when they report their suspicions, they do so at the risk of being sued for defamation of character.

Teachers are to make certain ALL students pass the state and federal mandated tests without regard to differences in ability, attendance, home environment, or ethnic background. They must communicate frequently with each student's parent by letter, phone, newsletter, memo, e-mail, and the progress report. (What's more...they had better temper honesty with political correctness when they do the reporting - if they want to keep their job.) And finally, teachers are expected to live their private lives as paragons of virtue so their students will be inspired to emulate their fine example. Whew! That's quite a demanding assignment.

Does every teacher live up to these lofty expectations? I'm afraid not. Does any teacher succeed in *all* of these areas? None that I know of. Although most teachers try to reach these lofty goals, they eventually learn that it is impossible to be all things to all kids and all parents, all of the time. Ultimately, more than a few decide teaching isn't for them.

The National Center of Education Statistics indicates that nationwide, 20 percent of new teachers leave the profession within three years of their first employment. The most often stated reasons for leaving are low salaries, student discipline issues, lack of community support, and a constant barrage of criticism regarding our American educational system.

But what about those brave and honorable souls who remain in the teaching profession? Why do they do it, and what kind of people are they? Most (perhaps, all) who make teaching a lifelong career do so because they love kids, they are committed to learning, and they believe they have a "calling." I realize that a "calling" sounds pretty corny, but it's true. Career teachers actually believe they make a difference in kids' lives, and they're willing to make sacrifices and endure some unpleasantness so that they can fulfill their mission.

And what is the real teacher like? The one who makes mistakes and endures criticism, but keeps coming back year after year? To find out, we'll look at the people who know the teacher best: His parents, spouse, kids, friends, community members, and students.

If you're a teacher's parent, you must learn how to build bookcases for your kid's classroom, save things such as wooden spools and empty toilet paper cylinders, and traipse all over the country gathering free "learning incentives" for your teacher-kid's students. Being the parent of a teacher is not an easy task.

For thirty-plus years my parents lived in Bonita Springs, Florida. The location made them an easy target for one of those annual, across-the-state pilgrimages designed to obtain learning incentives. I, along with four first-grade teaching colleagues, taught an ocean unit to about 150 students each year. We liked to "reward" our students with colorful brochures from Sea World at the end of the unit. One might think that the people in charge of promoting Sea World would absolutely jump at the chance to send 150 brochures to Independence, Iowa (population 7,000) every year. But no, that's not how it worked. Five brochures was the absolute limit! So, what were we supposed to do? Of course, there was only one solution.

I would ask mom and dad to drive the state of Florida every year and pick up free (usually a maximum of two per location) brochures, until they obtained the requested amount, and then mail them to me in Independence. And like most parents, they never refused. (They even pretended to enjoy their annual jaunt.)

After my father died, mom sold their home and moved to Mesa, Arizona where she could be close to my sister and other extended family. I think she figured she wouldn't have to drive across the state looking for Sea World brochures anymore. But, her assumption was only half right. Independence first grade teachers also taught an annual desert unit! (Happy touring, Mom.)

Now lets look at what it's like to be the spouse of a teacher. First of all, a teacher doesn't usually contribute buckets full of cash to the family coffers. Teaching salaries rank very near the bottom of the list when compared with other jobs that require the same (or less) amount of education. However, it isn't the amount of the paycheck that often causes friction in a teacher/non-teacher marriage. Instead, it is the way the teacher spends her paycheck.

Statistics show that the average teacher spends $600 of his own money for teaching materials, supplies, and classroom learning incentives. However, don't try to convince a teacher's spouse that his significant other's teaching related spending caps off at $600 a year. He'll blurt out a litany of items that will make your weekly grocery list look miniscule. Purchases like supplementary books and films to enhance a particular unit of study, posters, curtains, or other room enhancements. Throw in some room dividers, storage containers, portable fans, area rugs, file boxes, and a rocking chair. Don't forget the little extras they purchase in order to make a party special or help a disadvantaged student obtain some necessary school supplies. Oh well, most spouses of teachers understand that the vow of "...for richer or poorer" refers to the latter part of the equation.

And what does the teacher say when her spouse asks her to take a few days off without pay so that she can accompany him on a business trip? It often sounds something like this. "Honey, I'd just love to go, but I'm afraid that particular date is out of the question because the Iowa Test of Basic Skills is scheduled for those days. I couldn't possibly expect my kids to endure that experience with a substitute! Maybe next year."

Then there's the family vacation. First of all, the location usually needs to coincide with some unit the teacher-spouse covers in school and wants to learn more about. That wouldn't be so bad, if along the way she weren't forever yelling, "STOP! I just must take one (or thirty) of those little "thingies" back for my students." Golly, when you think about it, it's amazing that most teacher/non-teacher marriages survive!

Being a teacher's kid is not exactly a Sunday school picnic either. (Mark and Sean thought I didn't understand this, but I DID. I just never told them so.) The teacher-parent expects his own kid to set a good example in attendance, behavior, community service, politeness, and academic achievement. And those aren't the only challenges the teacher's kid faces. The kid of a teacher can't get away with any little misdeed at school. Why? Because some teacher always rats on him when he encounters the kid's parent (a colleague) in the faculty room or at a staff meeting.

Furthermore, the kid who has a teacher for a parent often doesn't have free reign to choose his own friends. Because teachers know (or know of) every kid in school, they think that entitles them to pick the "best" companions for their offspring. And of course that companion must be polite, considerate, trustworthy, academically focused, and on and on. Yes, all parents want their kids to have wholesome, honorable friends. But lets face it. When you don't have the opportunity to see a kid (or hear of his behavior) on a daily basis, you are forced to rely on our child's assessment of his friend and your own intuition. The teacher's kid misses that opportunity because a parent's observation overrides intuition.

And how about all that stuff you read concerning the importance of family togetherness? Well, if you're a teacher's kid, forget it. A teacher rarely leaves school at 4 o'clock or before. He has school meetings to attend, committees to chair, or class preparations to make. And what does he do after the dinner hour? He digs into a pile of term papers to correct, or starts work on the Progress Reports that are due at the end of the week.

Of course everyone knows teachers have "three months" off in the summer. Surely that must be a good time for teachers to bond with their own kids, right? Wrong. "Three months off" is strictly a myth. The school year normally ends in early June (with the exception of year-round schedules) and is followed by a few days of wrap-up time in the classroom. Shortly thereafter, most teachers enroll in a couple of summer workshops, and then take one or two post-graduate courses at a nearby college. When the calendar is turned to August, it's time to head back to the classroom to prepare for a new group of students. Three months? Try two weeks. Teachers' kids have to be content with quality time from their teacher-parent, 'cause there isn't a lot of quantity. Being a teacher's kid is not easy – but if given the opportunity, most wouldn't have it any other way.

What's it like to be a friend of a teacher? For starters, teachers never put you down. They insist on looking for the good in you, and they don't allow you to give up. When you invite your teacher-friend over for dinner and your meal ends up tasting like dog do-do, she'll simply say, "Your china is lovely." Then in her most encouraging voice she'll suggest that next time you fix a box of Kraft macaroni and cheese because she knows you'll do that perfectly! (Classroom habits practiced on a daily basis usually carry over into the real world.)

Have you ever attended a social event with a teacher? That almost always evolves into a "memorable" experience. When you arrive at your destination, your teacher-friend spots a parent of a former student. Boom. He excuses himself to inquire about the health and welfare of "his" kid, and that's the last you see of him for fifteen minutes. Later, he makes eye contact with an all-grown-up former student and off he goes for another half-hour. Yes, being the friend of a teacher can be "trying" at times – to say the least. Isn't it strange that many regard their teacher-friends as priceless treasures? (At least I sure hope they do!)

Every community has a large number of teachers. Most (unfortunately, not all) teachers are actively involved in the life of their community. What's it like to be on a committee with a teacher? Well, that can be a real challenge because teachers are so – well, so organized and so focused. Normally people go to committee meetings and sit around for a couple of hours grumbling about the various problems in their organization. Then they set a new meeting date, and head to their favorite watering hole for some R and R. But when a teacher is a member of the committee, everything changes. The teacher walks in promptly at 7:00 (they're never late) and announces that she absolutely must leave by 9:00 because she has papers to correct. Next she pulls out her yellow legal pad and says, "Let's write down our objectives so we don't get off track." Oh, my! Committee members do get more accomplished when a teacher is in their group, but they sure miss their whining time.

Students have the least to complain about when it comes to teachers. Kids are aware that teachers dress kind of goofy, and often drive the oldest cars in the parking lot. Kids know that teachers tell corny jokes, occasionally call them by the wrong name, and bug them about completing their assignments on time. Yes, kids know that teachers are far from perfect. But they also sense that a teacher's heart is in the right place.

They know that most teachers attempt to teach their subjects well, to be good role models, and to put their students' welfare at the top of their priority list. Kids understand that teachers respect them, have high aspirations for them, and will do everything in their power to help all of them become the best they can be. I guess it isn't a mere coincidence that most kids not only respect their teachers – they actually like them.

Now you know what real, living-breathing teachers are like. If at some point (like teacher-appreciation week or at the end of a school year) you think a certain teacher deserves a short verbal or written Thank You for going the extra mile – go right ahead and do it. But be prepared. If the teacher is a female, she will probably get all choked-up and teary eyed on you because she is unaccustomed to outward signs of appreciation. And if the teacher is a male, he might just blow his nose (really hard), and spend the next five minutes cleaning his glasses.

A teacher effects eternity; He can never tell where his influence stops.

- Henry Adams

30

"HE AIN'T HEAVY, FATHER..."

We are indeed fortunate to have millions of people in this country who contribute their time, money, and talent to help provide a quality education for kids. In this chapter I would like to acknowledge and say "thanks" to all of you who so eagerly and willingly give of yourselves for this purpose.

Teachers could not possibly educate our youth to their fullest potential if we had to do it alone. We need your input. We want your help. We value your suggestions. We appreciate your support.

Hilary Rodham Clinton (you remember, she's the one who "stood by her man" and more recently "explained" *why* in her $8 million dollar book) made popular the ancient African proverb that says, 'It takes a village to raise a child. Regardless of how you (or I) regard Ms. Clinton, she was right on the money with the slogan that helped put "her man" into the Oval Office. (We won't go into the business of what kept him there.)

Most of you don't stand on the sidelines and yell and chip and criticize and scream about our schools. You get in the game and contribute. When we win, you rejoice with us. When we lose, you respond with even greater effort. We take our hats off to you.

First I would like to address the people who have served or are currently serving on **Boards of Education**. You are perhaps the most maligned and misunderstood group of individuals that reside in any community. (Well, maybe it's a three-way tie between you, the City Council, and the local politicians.)

You attend meetings, study issues, formulate goals, appear at school functions, visit schools, hear complaints, field criticism, serve on committees, represent the public, act as a watchdog, and on and on. You do all of this on your own time and with no remuneration. All too often your only feedback is negative comments and critical letters-to-the-editor. You are the unsung heroes of our schools. Thank you, School Board Members.

Mentors. Webster's dictionary defines a mentor as, a "wise and faithful adviser or teacher." School mentors come in all sizes, colors, shapes, and ages. Some are male and some are female. Some are high school students, and some are senior citizens. Some are gorgeous to look at. Most are... well, just plain ordinary folk like you and I. All mentors are extremely valuable to both students and teachers.

Although policies vary from district to district, a typical mentoring arrangement finds a prescreened individual meeting alone with one student for approximately a half hour each week. These meetings are conducted at the school attendance center. Contact beyond the school building is allowed only with parental written consent, and is normally discouraged. Sometimes the mentoring partnership lasts a year, and other times it continues much longer. The mentor-student relationship begins when two strangers meet, and almost always evolves into a mutual bond of respect and friendship.

As mentors, you provide stability to a student's personal life. Through your unconditional acceptance, you enhance his self-concept. Through your commitment to serve, you become a role model on how to set goals and how to go about achieving them. You are your student's coach, advocate, and cheerleader. You are often his biggest fan. Working together, you make a great team.

As a teacher, it was neat to watch the positive bond that nearly always developed between a student and his mentor. The student watched the clock anxiously on his "mentor-visit" day. He could hardly wait! And judging by conversations with countless mentors, I believe most of them shared that same joyful anticipation.

Throughout my teaching career I had several occasions to share with a mentor some concerns I had regarding the behavior or achievement of the student that was being mentored. The mentor always listened, and invariably offered to help in any way possible. However, he also defended "his" kid as forcefully as a mother lion defends her cub. And that's okay. No, that's better than okay! Every kid needs an advocate. In some cases – with the exception of school personnel – the mentor is the child's only advocate. Thank you, Mentors.

PTA, Music Boosters, Drama and Speech Advocates, and Athletic Boosters. How could schools thrive or even survive without you? The answer is simple. They wouldn't. You do so much. You give unconditional support to the groups you represent. You conduct fund-raisers and you support the school staff in ways too numerous to list. You attend school-related events. You generously share your time, your money, and your talents. Thank you, "Student Boosters."

Business leaders. Where do teachers and students go every time they need funds to support some worthwhile school project that is in dire need of financial assistance? They come to you, their local business people. They understand that you have the same financial obligations as the rest of us, plus some. In addition to supporting yourself and your family, you have overhead to pay, losses to absorb, and the inevitable taxes. And what's more, many of you probably do not have "deep pockets." Still, we continue to ask for your help, and you continue to respond with an unqualified, "Yes." Thank you, Community Business Leaders.

Parents. I am not referring to you parents who support your own kids. You are expected to do that because that is your responsibility and it goes with the title of "parent." I am specifically speaking to the huge majority of you who support all kids.

During my tenure in the classroom I had the opportunity to watch you support whole classrooms and entire schools on hundreds of occasions and in a variety of ways. You help at holiday time. You assist the teacher on field trips. You furnish snacks for an entire room. You share printed materials and artifacts that relate to a particular unit of study. You explain or demonstrate a variety of skills and crafts. Sometimes you contribute funds to buy educational items for the classroom or help a disadvantaged child. Thank you, parents.

Last, but certainly not least, we owe a debt of gratitude to all of you people whom I will simply call "**Others**." You are the ones who come to school to read, to monitor special events, to demonstrate a particular area of expertise, or to assist the teacher in a project that needs multiple hands. You share pictures and memorabilia from far away places that you have visited. You serve on school-related committees, study groups, or organizations to promote the Arts. You attend school functions. You donate requested items needed by the school. You buy everything from light bulbs to pizza when a kid rings your doorbell and asks for a donation to help fund a particular school-related cause. You are the teacher's spouse who refrains from complaining when your mate spends countless hours of should-be-family-time, engaged in a *school*-related duty. Thank you, "Others."

A large framed poster from Boy's Town, Nebraska hangs in the family room of our home. The picture shows a small boy carrying another boy on his back during a blinding snowstorm. The young lad toting the load says, "He ain't heavy Father, ...he's m' brother." I believe that most of you consider every child to be your "brother", and you figuratively carry him on your back. You are the reason for the *one* set of footprints in the snow.

On behalf of teachers and administrators throughout this great land of ours, I want to thank you one and all. You truly are the "wind beneath our wings." We are thankful and proud to be members of a "village" that is united together for the purpose of educating children.

We are each of us angels with only one wing, and we can only fly by embracing one another.
-Luciano de Crescenzo

31

REFLECTIONS

The first and last day of every school year is an emotional roller coaster for kids, parents, and teachers. These two days prompt feelings that rival first day on the job jitters, wedding day doubts, first date expectations, and delivery room fears. Although emotions vary in type, intensity, and expression (depending on each individual's personality and prior experiences), everybody has them.

On the first day of a new school year parents rejoice in the fact that their childcare expenses will decrease. They worry about the effectiveness and the compassion of their kid's new teacher. They contemplate whether or not their youngster will fit in socially, and succeed academically. And they become nostalgic as they watch their offspring reach one more milestone on his way to independence and departure from the nest.

Kids are saddened by the passage of the carefree summer days that allowed them to sleep in, choose their own activities, and stay up late. They are excited to meet their new teacher and reconnect with old friends. They are fearful that they might look like a dork, say something stupid, or be the last one chosen for a team. They worry about whether or not their teacher will be mean, boring, judgmental, unfair, or downright nasty. And above all else, they hope their teacher will like them.

The first day of school also elicits strong emotions for the teacher (even on her forty-second year). She is excited to meet her new students. She is eager to share in their enthusiasm as they climb the next step of the education ladder. She wonders if this new class can possibly be as delightful as their predecessors were. She worries about whether or not she will be able to maintain discipline, have patience with the underachiever, challenge the gifted, please the parents, and ... the list goes on.

The last day of school is also charged with emotion for parents, kids, and teachers. But the feelings are quite different.

Parents are excited at the prospect of less-hectic schedules, the absence of homework supervision, and dealing with the complaints that accompany school attendance. They rejoice in the fact their youngster has successfully (more or less) completed another year. And they worry about how they will handle childcare for the summer, keep their child out of trouble and harm's way, and how to keep him from getting bored. (Frankly, I wouldn't spend a whole bunch of energy on the "bored" problem. Let the kid handle that one. It's *his* responsibility – not the parent's!)

Kids are excited about hundreds of things. They look forward to swimming, fishing, golf, tennis, digging up worms, and catching fireflies. They are anxious to sleep half the day, and stay up half the night. And perhaps surprisingly, more than a few experience some sadness on their last day of school. They will miss seeing their friends on a daily basis. They will miss the laughter, the camaraderie, the sharing, and the loyalty that has developed throughout the past year. And yes, most will miss their teacher.

Teachers are no exception when it comes to a mixed bag of emotions on the last day of school. They also anticipate sleeping past 6 a.m. and staying up late to watch Jay or David. They rejoice because they will not have to use their evenings and weekends to correct papers, plan units, or prepare report cards. They are gratified that every student made progress during the year, but worry about the kid who didn't achieve to his full potential. They revel in the fact they weren't hit with a lawsuit by an angry parent, but wonder why a minute number of parents remained aloof and/or uncooperative throughout the entire year. And finally, they offer Thanks for the very best class they ever had. They know there will never be another group that will steal their heart away like this group has. (Every class is unique, and every class makes an indelible mark on a teacher's heart.)

The last day of school presents an opportunity that is not there on the first day, or the one hundred and seventy nine days that follow. The last day allows school participants to look back and see all they have done, and examine everything they have learned during the past 180 days. The end of a school year is a time to reflect, and an experience to savor.

What did each group learn over the course of a year? Parents learned their preconceived notion of the "new" teacher was either right on the money, or was missed by a mile. They discovered they didn't always agree with the teacher's decisions or methods, but found her willing to listen to their concerns and work toward a resolution. They experienced situations where the teacher's motives were pure, but her tact was less than admirable. They learned the kid's version and teacher's version of an incident didn't always match. And they discovered that it often took some diligent sleuthing and a bit of soul searching to uncover the real story.

Parents learned that teachers aren't all the same. They have different personalities, talents, skills, and temperaments. They approach learning in different ways, tackle problems differently, and relate to kids with their own individual style. Hopefully, parents realized these differences were not synonymous with "good" or "bad," but with unique.

Jacquie McTaggart

Most parents came to the realization that his child's teacher went into the profession because he liked kids and felt he could make a positive difference in their lives. And that is the reason he has stayed there.

Kids probably learned the most throughout the course of a year, and only a portion of that knowledge involved subject matter. They learned that the school family was made up of a diverse and unique group. They learned how to accept and appreciate the kids who were different than they. They developed the skills of compromise and sharing that became bridges to peaceful solutions. They discovered most days were fun and exciting, but some were just plain dull and uneventful. (Notice, I did not say, "BORING!")

They discovered which buttons to push so their teacher would smile and say, "I'm so proud of you." And they learned which buttons *not* to push. Buttons that would provoke the teacher's "dirty look", a dreaded visit to the principal's office, or the life threatening "bad-news" telephone call to their parents.

Kids discovered that they and they alone were accountable for completing their assignments. They learned their teacher never bought into the "My *mom* forgot to put my book in the tote-bag" or "My dog ate my homework" stories.

Kids discovered their teachers were just ordinary mortals with the same assets and liabilities that every other human being has. They learned the teacher had his "good days" and his "bad days", and it didn't always correlate with the kids' achievement or behavior. They got to observe their teacher laugh, and on rare occasions they were forced to watch her cry. They noticed how the teacher didn't always know the answers, and how he sometimes made mistakes. They also witnessed the teacher say, "I was wrong. I'm sorry."

242

They saw up close and personal how their teacher was often unable to reach certain kids on a first, second or even third attempt. They also noticed she never gave up. They were fascinated to watch as the teacher searched for new and different ways to present the same old material in a more meaningful manner. They saw the teacher's excitement when the late bloomer exclaimed, "Ah-ha, now I understand!" And what's more, they felt the late bloomer's sense of accomplishment and they rejoiced for him.

And finally, each kid learned that his teacher was his friend. She was strict, but not mean spirited. She noticed his new haircut, fixed his "ouchies", laughed at his jokes, and empathized with his heartaches. She rejoiced in his successes, and provided encouragement when he experienced failure. She did not humiliate him, or allow others to do so. She liked to have fun and laugh and tease. She cared for him as a person. She will never forget him, and he knows it.

What do teachers learn and relearn year after year? They learn their students are powerful teachers. Kids teach them how to chuckle at the unexpected, and how to exercise restraint in moments of frustration. On a regular basis, students demonstrate the joy of making a new friend, and the sorrow that results from a damaged or broken friendship. Teachers learn from their students the excitement of a first snowfall, the wonderment of looking into a microscope for the first time, and the pain of watching a bird with an injured wing.

Teachers learn what love of family is by observing their students' joy and pride when Mom or Dad comes to the classroom door or attends a school function. Teachers learn that their students have the uncanny ability of transforming a yucky day into a "yippee" day by simply saying, "Oh, *that's* the way you do it!"

New teachers learn, and veteran teachers are reminded of the fact that there's no place they would rather be than with a classroom full of unique, unforgettable kids.

The writing of this book has been a labor of love for me. I would like to end it with an invitation. If you feel strongly about some issue that I have covered and would like to discuss it further, I'd love to hear from you. You may want to say, "YES! You told it the way it is." Or, you may want to tell me I am way off base on a particular topic and explain why you think so. Either way, I would enjoy hearing from you. I'm always willing to listen to differing opinions. And who knows? I just might be propelled into writing, *More From the Teacher's Desk.* My email address is mctag@indytel.com. If you do contact me, please be gentle. I cry easily!

When I look at a patch of dandelions, I see a bunch of weeds that are going to take over my yard.

Kids see flowers for Mom and blowing white fluff they can wish on.

When I look at an old drunk and he smiles at me, I see a smelly, dirty person who probably wants money – and I look away.

Kids see someone smiling at them, and they smile back.

When I hear music I love, I know I can't carry a tune and don't have much rhythm – so I sit self-consciously and listen.

Kids feel the beat and move to it. They sing out the words. If they don't know them, they make up their own.

When I feel wind on my face, I brace myself against it. I feel it messing up my hair and pulling me back when I walk.

Kids close their eyes, spread their arms and fly with it, until they fall to the ground laughing.

When I pray, I say thee and thou and grant me this, give me that.

Kids say, "Hi God! Thanks for my toys and my friends. Please keep the bad dreams away tonight. Sorry, I don't want to go to Heaven yet. I would miss my Mommy and Daddy."

When I see a mud puddle I step around it. I see muddy shoes and dirty carpets.

Kids sit in it. They see dams to build, rivers to cross, and worms to play with.

I wonder if we are given kids to teach or to learn from?

-Author Unknown

I wish you Big Mud Puddles and Sunny Yellow Dandelions!!!

Printed in the United States
20117LVS00003B/58-510